"This lovely, easy-to-read primer by Dane Ortlund grounds our discipleship in the glowing center of Christianity—our Lord Jesus. It's easy to think that as we grow as Christians, we move on to 'higher things' (whatever that means!), when in fact we simply need to learn the beauty and depth of Jesus and all that he's done for us. That's what Ortlund helps us do here. This book will bless you!"

Paul E. Miller, author, *A Praying Life* and *J-Curve: Dying and Rising with Jesus in Everyday Life*

"That angst in your soul for more is a part of the growing process—a gift of hunger and thirst that Jesus, the inexhaustible well, will fill. In *Deeper*, Dane Ortlund reminds us that the angst is satisfied not by behavioral modification or some quick fix but by the beauty of friendship with Jesus and the peace more deeply accepted in our souls. If you are hungry and thirsty for more life, more joy, more peace, and more Jesus, this is a book for you."

Matt Chandler, Lead Pastor, The Village Church, Dallas, Texas; President, Acts 29 Church Planting Network; author, *The Mingling of Souls* and *The Explicit Gospel*

"Jesus said that our greatest 'work' is to believe. As much as any living author, Dane Ortlund has helped me to believe again by reacquainting me with the stunning tenderness and beauty of Jesus. As I read his words, I can sense my heart growing in trust, devotion, and godly affections, grounded in the Savior's love for me. In this incredibly helpful, pastoral book, Dane works out the implications of that vision of Jesus for personal growth, showing us how the key to going further with Jesus is going deeper in his finished work."

J. D. Greear, Lead Pastor, The Summit Church, Raleigh-Durham, North Carolina

"Having marinated in the wisdom, beauty, and encouragement of Dane's new book, I totally understand why my friend chose *deeper* as the primary image for the title. How does God change us as his beloved daughters and sons? Think less of climbing a mountain and more of swimming in a deep ocean of the always-more-ness of Jesus. If you've ever wondered what the Bible really means by 'fixing our gaze on Jesus, the author and perfecter of our faith,' this should be the next book you spend time with. Dane helps us understand that the gospel is more of a person to adore and know than theological propositions and categories to master."

Scotty Smith, Pastor Emeritus, Christ Community Church, Franklin, Tennessee; Teacher in Residence, West End Community Church, Nashville, Tennessee

DEEPER

Union

A book series edited by Michael Reeves

Rejoice and Tremble: The Surprising Good News of the Fear of the Lord, Michael Reeves (2021)

What Does It Mean to Fear the Lord?, Michael Reeves (2021, concise version of *Rejoice and Tremble*)

Deeper: Real Change for Real Sinners, Dane C. Ortlund (2021)

How Does God Change Us?, Dane C. Ortlund (2021, concise version of *Deeper*)

DEEPER

Real Change for Real Sinners

DANE C. ORTLUND

WHEATON, ILLINOIS

Library of Congress Cataloging-in-Publication Data
Names: Ortlund, Dane Calvin, author.
Title: Deeper : real change for real sinners / Dane C. Ortlund.
Description: Wheaton, Illinois : Crossway, 2021. | Series: Union | Includes bibliographical references and index.
Identifiers: LCCN 2021002495 (print) | LCCN 2021002496 (ebook) | ISBN 9781433573996 (hardcover) | ISBN 9781433574009 (pdf) | ISBN 9781433574016 (mobi) | ISBN 9781433574023 (epub)
Subjects: LCSH: Sanctification—Christianity. | Spiritual formation.
Classification: LCC BT765 .O78 2021 (print) | LCC BT765 (ebook) | DDC 234/.8—dc23
LC record available at https://lccn.loc.gov/2021002495
LC ebook record available at https://lccn.loc.gov/2021002496

*Affectionately dedicated to
the faculty of Covenant Theological Seminary, 2002–2006,
who taught me about real change from the Bible,
then showed me with their lives*

"Aslan," said Lucy, "you're bigger."

"That is because you are older, little one," answered he.

"Not because you are?"

"I am not. But every year you grow, you will find me bigger."

C. S. LEWIS, *Prince Caspian*

Contents

Series Preface

OUR INNER CONVICTIONS AND VALUES shape our lives and our ministries. And at Union—the cooperative ministries of Union School of Theology, Union Publishing, Union Research, and Union Mission (visit www.theolo.gy)—we long to grow and support men and women who will delight in God, grow in Christ, serve the church, and bless the world. This Union series of books is an attempt to express and share those values.

They are values that flow from the beauty and grace of God. The living God is so glorious and kind, he cannot be known without being adored. Those who truly know him will love him, and without that heartfelt delight in God, we are nothing but hollow hypocrites. That adoration of God necessarily works itself out in a desire to grow in Christlikeness. It also fuels a love for Christ's precious bride, the church, and a desire humbly to serve—rather than use—her. And, lastly, loving God brings us to share his concerns, especially to see his life-giving glory fill the earth.

Each exploration of a subject in the Union series will appear in two versions: a full volume and a concise one. The idea is that church leaders can read the full treatment, such as this one, and so delve into each topic while making the more accessible concise version widely available to their congregations.

My hope and prayer is that these books will bless you and your church as you develop a deeper delight in God that overflows in joyful integrity, humility, Christlikeness, love for the church, and a passion to make disciples of all nations.

Michael Reeves
SERIES EDITOR

Introduction

The question itself immediately elicits different feelings among us. Some of us feel guilt. We're not growing, and we know it. And the guilt is itself self-perpetuating, further paralyzing us in spiritual stagnation.

For others of us, longing erupts. We deeply desire to grow more than we are.

Some of us, if we're honest, become smug when the question of spiritual growth arises. We are pretty confident we're doing fine, though this self-assessment is largely shaped by quietly comparing ourselves with others, and a less-than-penetrating understanding of what really motivates us in our Christian lives.

The question ignites low-grade cynicism for others of us. We've tried. Or at least it seems that way. We've attempted this strategy and that one, read this book and that, been to this conference and that. And at the end of the day, we still feel like we're spinning our wheels, unable to get real traction in our growth in grace.

None of us questions the need to grow. We see it in the Bible: "Grow in the grace and knowledge of our Lord and Savior Jesus Christ" (2 Pet. 3:18). "We are to grow up in every way" (Eph. 4:15). And we see the need for growth not only in the Bible but in our own hearts. The painful exercise of honest self-examination surprises us. We discover that so much of our lives, so much even of the ways we are blessing the world around us, flows subtly from the fountain of Self. The gift is given, the service is rendered, the sacrifice is made, not out of the large-hearted motives we present to others, and to God, and even to ourselves, but for self-serving purposes. And that's only considering what others see. What about the ugliness of our lives when no one's looking? How do we kill the sins done in the dark?

The question, then, isn't *whether* we need to grow but how. And for everyone who has been born again, somewhere amid these diverse reactions there will always be a seed of sincere desire for growth.

How then does it happen?

The basic point of this book is that change is a matter of going deeper. Some believers think change happens through outward improvement—behaving more and more in accord with some moral norm (the biblical law, or the commands of Jesus, or conscience, or whatever). Others think change happens mainly through intellectual addition—understanding doctrine with greater breadth and precision. Others think it comes centrally through felt experience—sensory increase as we worship God.

My argument is that all three of these elements are included in healthy Christian development (and if any is missing, we are out of proportion and will not grow), but real growth transcends them all. Growing in Christ is not centrally improving or adding or experiencing but *deepening*. Implicit in the notion of deepening is that you already have what you need. Christian growth is bringing what you do and say and even feel into line with what, in fact, you already are.

This is roughly the way Henry Scougal outlined the Christian life in his little book *The Life of God in the Soul of Man*.[1] Scougal was a professor of divinity at the University of Aberdeen who died of tuberculosis at age twenty-eight. In 1677 he wrote a lengthy letter to a discouraged friend which later became the book. It was the catalyst in the conversion of British evangelist George Whitefield, who said, "I never knew what true religion was till God sent me this excellent treatise."[2] In that book Scougal says that some Christians think we grow through purer behavior, others through sharper doctrine, and others through richer emotions, but real change occurs through this reality: the life of God in the soul of man.

Scougal and other saints from the past will help us climb inside the Bible and see the riches that God has for us in his word for our day-to-day Christian lives. And we will bring to the table various sages from the past to help us really understand the Scriptures. The vast majority of wisdom available to us today is found among the dead. Though their spirits are now with Christ in heaven, the books and sermons of Augustine, Gregory the Great, Luther, Calvin, Knox, Sibbes, Goodwin, Owen, Bunyan, Edwards, Whitefield, Ryle, Spurgeon, Bavinck, Lewis, and Lloyd-Jones remain with us. So we will draw strength and insight from the great ones of the past far more than the famous ones of the present as we consider what Scripture gives us for growing in Christ.

And so we will be thinking in this book about "real change for real sinners," as our subtitle puts it—as opposed to surface change for

---

1   Henry Scougal, *The Life of God in the Soul of Man* (Fearn, Ross-shire, Scotland: Christian Focus, 1996).
2   In Thomas S. Kidd, *George Whitefield: America's Spiritual Founding Father* (New Haven, CT: Yale University Press, 2014), 28.

theoretical sinners. We're not after behavior modification in this book. I'm not going to talk to you about setting your alarm earlier or cutting carbs. We're not even going to reflect on tithing or church attendance or journaling or small groups or taking the sacraments or reading the Puritans. All of that can be done out of rottenness of heart. We're talking about *real* change. And we're talking about real change for *real sinners*. If you confess the doctrine of original sin but at the same time feel yourself to be doing pretty well as a Christian, you can put this book back on the shelf. This book is for the frustrated. The exhausted. Those on the brink. Those on the verge of giving up any real progress in their Christian growth. If you not only subscribe to the doctrine of original sin on paper but also find yourself proving the doctrine of original sin in your daily life, this book is for you.

A few things right up front.

First, I'm not going to hurry you. No one else should either. We are complicated sinners. Sometimes we take two steps forward and three steps back. We need time. Be patient with yourself. A sense of urgency, yes; but not a sense of hurry. Overnight transformations are the exception, not the norm. Slow change is still real change. And it's the normal way God deals with us. Take your time.

Second, as you begin this book, open your heart to the possibility of real change in your life. One of the devil's great victories is to flood our hearts with a sense of futility. Perhaps his greatest victory in your life is not a sin you are habitually committing but simply a sense of helplessness as to real growth.

Third, I encourage you not to consume this book but to reflect your way through it. Maybe that means journaling alongside reading. Maybe it means reading with a friend. Do whatever you can to process slowly, marinating, meditating, letting the Bible's truths shepherd you into the green pastures you long for in your walk with the Lord. Fast reading, for a book like this, is minimally absorbing reading.

Fourth, this book is written by a fellow patient, not a doctor. It is written to me as much as by me. Out of failure as much as out of success.

1

Jesus

THIS IS A BOOK ABOUT GROWING IN CHRIST. The first thing to
get clear, then, is what Jesus Christ himself is like. Our growth is
not independent personal improvement. It is growth *in Christ*. Who
then is he?

The temptation for many of us at this point is to assume we pretty
much know what Jesus is like. We've been saved by him. We've spent
time in the Bible over the years. We've read some books about him.
We've told a few others about him.

And yet, if we are honest, we still find our lives riddled with failure
and worry and dysfunction and emptiness.

One common reason we fail to leave sin behind is that we have
a domesticated view of Jesus. Not a heterodox view; we are fully
orthodox in our Christology. We understand that he came from
heaven as the Son of God to live the life we cannot live and die
the death we deserve to die. We affirm his glorious resurrection.
We confess with the ancient creeds that he is truly God and truly
man. We don't have a heterodox view. We have a domesticated
view that, for all its doctrinal precision, has downsized the glory
of Christ in our hearts.

So we need to begin by getting clear on who this person is in whom we grow. And we start just there—he is a person. Not just a historical figure, but an actual person, alive and well today. He is to be related to. Trusted, spoken to, listened to. Jesus is not a concept. Not an ideal. Not a force. Growing in Christ is a relational, not a formulaic, experience.

Who then is this person?

Unsearchable

Ephesians speaks of "the unsearchable riches of Christ" (Eph. 3:8). The Greek word underlying "unsearchable" occurs just one other time in the New Testament, in Romans 11:33: "Oh, the depth of the riches and wisdom and knowledge of God! How unsearchable are his judgments and how *inscrutable* his ways!" Romans 11 calls God's wisdom and knowledge unsearchable. That makes sense. God is infinite and omniscient; of course his wisdom and knowledge are unsearchable. But Ephesians 3 calls Christ's *riches* unsearchable. How so? What does it mean that there are riches in Christ and that these riches are unsearchable? That we can dig and dig but never hit bottom on them?

As you wade into this book, let me propose an idea. Let me suggest that you consider the possibility that your current mental idea of Jesus is the tip of the iceberg. That there are wondrous depths to him, realities about him, still awaiting your discovery. I'm not disregarding the real discipleship already at play in your life and the true discoveries of the depths of Jesus Christ you have already made. But let me ask you to open yourself up to the possibility that one reason you see modest growth and ongoing sin in your life—if that is indeed the case—is that the Jesus you are following is a junior varsity Jesus, an unwittingly reduced Jesus, an unsurprising and predictable Jesus. I'm not assuming that's the case. I'm just asking you to test yourself, with honesty.

When Christopher Columbus reached the Caribbean in 1492, he named the natives "Indians," thinking he had reached what Europeans of the time referred to as "the Indies" (China, Japan, and India). In fact he was nowhere close to South or East Asia. In his path were vast regions of land, unexplored and uncharted, of which Columbus knew nothing. He assumed the world was smaller than it was.

Have we made a similar mistake with regard to Jesus Christ? Are there vast tracts of who he is, according to biblical revelation, that are unexplored? Have we unintentionally reduced him to manageable, predictable proportions? Have we been looking at a junior varsity, decaffeinated, one-dimensional Jesus of our own making, thinking we're looking at the real Jesus? Have we snorkeled in the shallows, thinking we've now hit bottom on the Pacific?

In this chapter I'd like to mention seven facets of Christ, seven "regions" of Christ that may be under-explored in our generation. Dozens more could be considered. But we'll restrict ourselves to these seven: ruling, saving, befriending, persevering, interceding, returning, and tenderness. The point of this exercise is to bring the living Christ himself into sharper, starker contrast, to see him loom larger and more radiant and more glorious than ever before—to trade in our snorkel and face mask for scuba gear that takes us down into depths we've never peered into before—and to seek Christian growth out of an accurate and ever-deepening vision of the Christ to whom we have been united.

Ruling

Jesus exercises supreme authority over the entire universe.

Just before his ascension he said, "All authority in heaven and on earth has been given to me" (Matt. 28:18). He is not hoping to be in charge; he rules supremely now. The world's sidelining of his authority does nothing to reflect the reality of that authority. From heaven's perspective, everything is going according to plan. Jesus Christ is overseeing all that happens, both in the church and in world history at large. Our perception of and ability to see his rule may wax and wane; but that's perception only. His actual rule holds steady—supreme, strong, exhaustive, all-seeing. No drug deal goes down apart from his awareness, no political scandal unfolds beyond the reach of his vision, no injustice can be exacted behind his back. When today's world leaders gather together, they themselves are held in the hand of a risen Galilean carpenter.

This supreme reign holds true not only for the cosmos and for world history but also for your own little life. He sees you. He knows you. Nothing is hid from his gaze. You will be judged one day not according to what was visible to others but according to what you really were and did. The Bible says that when Jesus comes to judge the world, he "will bring to light the things now hidden in darkness and will disclose the purposes of the heart" (1 Cor. 4:5). Not only what we did in secret, but even our very motives will be laid bare and judged.

We may not see Jesus with our eyes. But he is the most real thing in the universe. The Bible says that "in him all things hold together" (Col. 1:17). Subtract Jesus from the universe, and everything falls apart. He is not a bobblehead Savior, to be smiled at and merely added to an otherwise well-oiled life. He is the mighty sustainer of the universe, to whose supreme rule we will bow the knee in either this life or the next (Phil. 2:10).

Consider the depiction of him in Revelation 1. John is clearly attempting to capture in words what cannot be captured in words as he describes

one like a son of man, clothed with a long robe and with a golden
sash around his chest. The hairs of his head were white, like white
wool, like snow. His eyes were like a flame of fire, his feet were like
burnished bronze, refined in a furnace, and his voice was like the
roar of many waters. In his right hand he held seven stars, from
his mouth came a sharp two-edged sword, and his face was like
the sun shining in full strength. When I saw him, I fell at his feet
as though dead. (Rev. 1:13–17)

Have you reduced the Lord Jesus to a safe, containable, predictable
Savior who pitches in and helps out your otherwise smoothly running
existence? Have you treated what is spiritually nuclear as a double-A
battery? Might one reason we stall out in our growth in Christ be that
we have unwittingly domesticated the expansive authority and rule of
Jesus Christ over all things? Might we be lacking an appropriate fear
of, wonder at, trembling before, the Lord Jesus, the real Jesus who will
one day silence the raging of the nations with a moment's whisper?
Jesus rules.

Saving

It may seem obvious that the real Jesus is a saving Jesus. But I mean
something quite specific when I call him "saving." I mean he is saving *and not only helping.* As sinners we are not wounded but dead in
our trespasses and we need not merely strengthening or helping but
resurrection, a full-scale deliverance (Eph. 2:1–6).

As we consider our growth in Christ, do we have an impoverished
view of the length to which God had to go in Christ to deliver us?
And in our ongoing walk with the Lord now, do we functionally
believe that the healthy Christian life is basically a matter of our efforts, baptized with a little extra push from Jesus?

Do we know what it means to be *saved*? In Luke's Gospel, Jesus tells a parable to make the point:

One of the Pharisees asked him to eat with him, and he went into the Pharisee's house and reclined at table. And behold, a woman of the city, who was a sinner, when she learned that he was reclining at table in the Pharisee's house, brought an alabaster flask of ointment, and standing behind him at his feet, weeping, she began to wet his feet with her tears and wiped them with the hair of her head and kissed his feet and anointed them with the ointment. Now when the Pharisee who had invited him saw this, he said to himself, "If this man were a prophet, he would have known who and what sort of woman this is who is touching him, for she is a sinner." And Jesus answering said to him, "Simon, I have something to say to you." And he answered, "Say it, Teacher."

"A certain moneylender had two debtors. One owed five hundred denarii, and the other fifty. When they could not pay, he cancelled the debt of both. Now which of them will love him more?" Simon answered, "The one, I suppose, for whom he cancelled the larger debt." And he said to him, "You have judged rightly." Then turning toward the woman he said to Simon, "Do you see this woman? I entered your house; you gave me no water for my feet, but she has wet my feet with her tears and wiped them with her hair. You gave me no kiss, but from the time I came in she has not ceased to kiss my feet. You did not anoint my head with oil, but she has anointed my feet with ointment. Therefore I tell you, her sins, which are many, are forgiven—for she loved much. But he who is forgiven little, loves little." And he said to her, "Your sins are forgiven." Then those who were at table with him began to say among themselves, "Who is this, who even forgives sins?" And he said to the woman, "Your faith has saved you; go in peace." (Luke 7:36–50)

Every human is five hundred denarii in debt. The point of the parable is that we tend to *feel* only fifty denarii in debt. The more obvious failures of a given culture sense their sinfulness more readily than others and are therefore readier and more eager for a deliverance that sweeps them up out of death with a full and total salvation.

One reason our spiritual growth grinds down is that we gradually lose a heart sense of the profound length to which Jesus went to save us. *Save* us. When we were running full speed the other direction, he chased us down, subdued our rebellion, and opened our eyes to see our need of him and his all-sufficiency to meet that need. We were not drowning, in need of being thrown a life-preserver; we were stone-dead at the bottom of the ocean. He pulled us up, breathed new life into us, and set us on our feet—and every breath we now draw is owing to his full and utter deliverance of us in all our helplessness and death.

Jesus saves.

Befriending

"No longer do I call you servants . . . but I have called you friends" (John 15:15). A heart sense of the friendship of Jesus with his own is a facet of his all-sufficiency without which vital growth cannot happen.

Some of us may have a strong sense of the transcendent glory of Jesus—as vital an aspect of who he is as any. We tremble at the thought of him. His resplendent greatness looms over our daily consciousness. We approach him with reverence and awe. As we should!

But he who is both Lion and Lamb is both transcendent and immanent, both far and near, both great and good—both King and Friend. I am asking you whether the Savior is your dearest and truest *friend*.

What does a friend do? A friend draws near in time of need. A friend delights to come into solidarity with us, bearing our burdens. A friend listens. A friend is available to us, never too high or important to give us time.

A friend shares his deepest heart. That's precisely the point of the above quote from John 15, which more fully reads, "No longer do I call you servants, for the servant does not know what his master is doing; but I have called you friends, for all that I have heard from my Father I have made known to you" (John 15:15). Incredible: the triune God brings us into his plans to restore the universe. He makes us part of his inner circle. He informs us of what he is doing and welcomes our participation in it.

Jesus was accused of being "a friend of tax collectors and sinners" (Matt. 11:19; Luke 7:34). Yet that very accusation, laced with contempt, is deep comfort to those who know that they fall into that category of "sinners." That is why these two groups (tax collectors and sinners) were precisely those who "were all drawing near to hear him" in Luke 15:1. Around Jesus, sinners—those who *know* themselves to be sinners—feel safe. They find themselves both known to be guilty and embraced in love, rather than one or the other. Our felt shame is what draws Jesus in. He is the mighty friend of sinners.

And what other kind of Savior will do? Who of us could really get fresh traction in our lives if we were following a Savior who kept at a safe distance? Who treated us not like friends but like employees? But if this is a Savior who draws near to us, who is repelled only by self-righteousness but never by acknowledged shame and weakness, there is no limit to just how deep a transformation is possible in us. It is at our point of deepest guilt and regret that his friendship embraces us most assuredly, most steadfastly.

If he is the friend of sinners, and if you know yourself to be a sinner, then let him befriend you more deeply than you ever have. Open up to him as you do to no other earthly friend. Let him love you as the friend of failures, the invincible ally of the weak.

Jesus befriends us.

Persevering

It is the nature of all human relationships that they vacillate. We profess undying commitment to each other, and we truly mean it. But we humans are fickle. Even in marriage, we enter in by force of a covenant. Why? Because we know our feelings come and go. We need a bond that goes deeper than our feelings to bind husband and wife together.

Who is Jesus? A non-vacillating friend. He perseveres. Heading into the final week of his earthly life, John's Gospel tells us, "having loved his own who were in the world, he loved them to the end" (John 13:1). Jesus binds himself to his people. No expiration date. No end of the road. Our side of the commitment will falter and stumble, but his never does.

We will not grow in Christ if we view his presence and favor as a ticking clock, ready for an alarm to go off once we fail him enough. We can flourish into deeper health only as the truth settles over us that once Jesus has brought us to himself, he will never be looking for an off-ramp. He will stick by us to the end. In that knowledge we calm down and begin to flourish. One Bible scholar rightly called our growth in Christ "a strangely relaxed kind of strenuousness."[1] We strain forward, but it is a straining that is at the same time relaxed,

---

1 C. F. D. Moule, "'The New Life' in Colossians 3:1–17," *Review and Expositor* 70, no. 4 (1973): 482.

because it has been settled in our hearts that we cannot sin our way out of the grip of Jesus.

That's the logic of Romans 5. Jesus died for us "while we were still weak" (v. 6), "while we were enemies" (v. 10)—he certainly isn't going to let us go now that we are his brothers. If Jesus went to the cross for us when we did not belong to him, he has proven that he will hang in there with us now that we do.

Jesus perseveres with us.

Interceding

Another vital yet neglected part of our growth in Christ is knowing that his work did not end when we rose from the dead. It is common but mistaken to limit the work of Christ to

birth → life → death → burial → resurrection → ascension.

But this leaves off the part of his work that he is doing right now:

birth → life → death → burial → resurrection → ascension → intercession.

The Bible says that no one can condemn believers because "Christ Jesus is the one . . . who is at the right hand of God, who indeed is interceding for us" (Rom. 8:34). He is speaking up for us. *Jesus prays for us.* This is what the ascended Christ does. The old theologian Thomas Goodwin said, "Let me tell you, he would still be preaching this day, but he had other business to do for you in heaven, where he is now praying and interceding for you, even when you are sinning; as on earth we see he did for the Jews when they were a-crucifying him."[2]

2 Thomas Goodwin, *Encouragements to Faith*, in *The Works of Thomas Goodwin*, 12 vols. (repr., Grand Rapids, MI: Reformation Heritage, 2006), 4:224.

Jesus is not bored in heaven. He is fully engaged on our behalf, as engaged as ever he was on earth. He is interceding for us. Why? Because we continue to sin *as believers*. If conversion so changed us that we never sinned again, we would not need Christ's intercessory work. We would only need his death and resurrection to pay for our pre-conversion sins. But he is a comprehensive Savior. His present intercessory work applies his past atoning work moment-by-moment before the Father as we move through life desiring to please the Lord but often failing. The Bible says that Jesus "is able to save to the uttermost those who draw near to God through him, since he always lives to make intercession for them" (Heb. 7:25). His speaking on our behalf in the courts of heaven is a constant, abiding reality—"he always lives to make intercession."

We will grow in Christ only as we recognize the ally Jesus Christ is to us, now in heaven. He did not die and rise again on our behalf back then only to stand now with arms crossed seeing how we'll do in response. He continues to work on our behalf—he goes "to the uttermost" for us—advocating for us when no one else will, not even we ourselves. *He is more committed to your growth in him than you are.*

Jesus intercedes.

Returning

Our growth in Christ also draws strength from a vivid heart sense of his imminent return.

It is hard to move forward in the Christian life if we allow ourselves to be lulled into the monotonous sense that this world will simply roll on forever as it currently is. But as we foster an expectation of the time "when the Lord Jesus is revealed from heaven with his mighty angels in flaming fire" (2 Thess. 1:7–8), urgency and expectancy spur us forward.

Do we really believe that one day, "in that resurrection morning," as Jonathan Edwards preached in 1746, "when the Sun of Righteousness shall appear in the heavens, shining in all his brightness and glory, he will come forth as a bridegroom, he shall come in the glory of his Father, with all his holy angels"?[3] Consider it: This is going to happen on an actual day in world history. A certain month, a certain date. It has been fixed (Acts 17:31). Only God knows (Matt. 24:36). But it is imminent (Matt. 24:42). When it happens, will we not lament our complacency about growing in Christ? Will we not be mystified at how our bank accounts and reputations loomed so large in our minds, so much larger than our actual spiritual conditions?

Jesus left this earth quietly, but he will return loudly (1 Thess. 4:16). He slipped away; but he will come roaring back. It may be tomorrow. Even if not, we're one day closer.

Jesus is returning.

Tender

Finally—and this is what I want ringing in your heart most strongly as you continue through the rest of this book—Jesus is infinitely tender.

He is the most open and accessible, the most peaceful and accommodating person in the universe. He is the gentlest, least abrasive person you will ever experience. Infinite strength, infinite meekness. Dazzlingly resplendent; endlessly calm.

If you had only a few words to define who Jesus is, what would you say? In the one place where he himself tells us about his own heart, he says, "I am gentle and lowly in heart" (Matt. 11:29). And remember

---

3 Jonathan Edwards, "The Church's Marriage to Her Sons, and to Her God," in *The Works of Jonathan Edwards*, vol. 25, *Sermons and Discourses, 1743–1758*, ed. Wilson H. Kimnach (New Haven, CT: Yale University Press, 2006), 183.

that the "heart" in biblical terms is not merely our emotions but the innermost animating center of all that we do. Our deepest loves and desires and ambitions pour out of our hearts. And when Jesus opens himself up and tells us of the fountain, the engine, the throbbing core of all that he does, he says that deeper than anything else, he is gentle and lowly. Peer down into the deepest recesses of Jesus Christ and there we find: gentleness and lowliness.

We who know our hearts resist this. We see the ugliness within. We can hardly face ourselves, we feel so inadequate. And Jesus is perfectly holy, the divine Son of God. It is normal and natural, even in our churches, to sense instinctively that he is holding his people at arm's length. This is why we need a Bible. The testimony of the entire Bible, culminating in Matthew 11:29, is that God defies what we instinctively feel by embracing his people in their mess. He finds penitence, distress, need, and lack irresistible.

You don't have to go through security to get to Jesus. You don't have to get in line or take a ticket. No waving for his attention. No raising your voice to make sure he hears you.

In your smallness, he notices you. In your sinfulness, he draws near to you. In your anguish, he is in solidarity with you.

What we must see is not only that Jesus is gentle toward you but that he is positively drawn toward you when you are most sure he doesn't want to be. It's not only that he is not repelled by your fallenness—he finds your need and emptiness and sorrow irresistible. He is not slow to meet you in your need. It's the difference between a teenager's alarm going off on a Monday morning, forcing him to drag himself out of bed, and that same teen springing out of bed on Christmas morning. Just look at the Savior in Matthew, Mark, Luke, and John. With whom does he hang out? What draws forth his tears? What gets him out of bed in the morning? With whom does he eat lunch? The sidelined, the hollowed out, those long out of hope, those who have sent their lives into meltdown.

The first thing I want to make clear here, early in this book, is that the real Jesus is gentle and lowly in heart. I say the *real* Jesus because we all unwittingly dilute him. We cut him down to what our minds can naturally imagine. But the Bible corrects us, tells us to stop doing that. We can only create a Jesus in our own image—a Jesus of moderate gentleness and mercy—without a Bible. Scripture tears down that diluted Jesus and lets loose the real Christ. And what we find is that his deepest heart is gentle and lowly.

This is a book about how we change. Let me be plain. *You will not change until you get straight who Jesus is, particularly with regard to his surprising tenderness.* And then spend your whole life long going deeper into the gentleness of Jesus. The only alternative to the real Jesus is to get back on the treadmill—the treadmill of doing your best to follow and honor Jesus but believing his mercy and grace to be a stockpile gradually depleted by your failures, and hoping to make it to death before the mountain of mercy runs out. Here is the teaching of the Bible: If you are in Christ, your sins cause that stockpile to grow all the more. Where sins abound, his grace superabounds. It is in your pockets of deepest shame and regret that his heart dwells *and won't leave.*

As you read this book and as you continue to work your way through life, shed once and for all the reduced Jesus and lift your eyes to the real Jesus, the Jesus whose tenderness ever outstrips and embraces your weaknesses, the Christ whose riches are unsearchable. This Christ is one under whose care and instruction you will finally be able to blossom and grow.

"I am gentle and lowly in heart."

Jesus is tender.

The Real Christ

Make your growth journey a journey into Christ himself. Explore uncharted regions of who he is. Resist the tendency we all have to whittle him down to our preconceived expectation of what he must be like. Let him surprise you. Let his fullness arrest you and buoy you along. Let him be a big Christ. C. S. Lewis remarked in a 1959 letter:

> "Gentle Jesus," my elbow! The most striking thing about Our Lord is the union of great ferocity with extreme tenderness. (Remember Pascal? "I do not admire the extreme of one virtue unless you show me at the same time the extreme of the opposite virtue. One shows one's greatness not by being at an extremity but by being simultaneously at two extremities and filling all the space between.")
>
> Add to this that He is also a supreme ironist, dialectician, and (occasionally) humourist. So go on! You are on the right track now: getting to the real Man behind all the plaster dolls that have been substituted for Him. This is the appearance in Human form of the God who made the Tiger *and* the Lamb, the avalanche *and* the rose. He'll frighten and puzzle you: but the real Christ *can* be loved and admired as the doll can't.[4]

Determine today, before God, through the Bible and good books explaining it, that you will spend the rest of your life wading into the unsearchable riches of the real Christ.

Let him, in all his endless fullness, love you into growth.

---

4 C. S. Lewis, *The Collected Letters of C. S. Lewis*, vol. 3, *Narnia, Cambridge, and Joy, 1950–1963*, ed. Walter Hooper (San Francisco: HarperCollins, 2009), 1011; emphasis original.

2

Despair

THERE IS A STRANGE THOUGH CONSISTENT MESSAGE throughout the Bible. We are told time and again that the way forward will feel like we're going backward.

The Psalms tell us that those whose hearts are breaking and who feel crushed by life are the people God is closest to (Ps. 34:18). Proverbs tells us it is to the low and the destitute that God shows favor (Prov. 3:34). In Isaiah we are surprised to learn that God dwells in two places: way up high, in the glory of heaven, and way down low, with those void of self-confidence and empty of themselves (Isa. 57:15; 66:1–2). Jesus tells us that "unless a grain of wheat falls into the earth and dies, it remains alone; but if it dies, it bears much fruit" (John 12:24). He tells us that the way to greatness is service and the way to be first is to be everyone's slave (Mark 10:43–44). James has the audacity to instruct us, "Let your laughter be turned to mourning" (James 4:9).

Why does the Bible do this? Does God want us always feeling bad about ourselves? Is he eager to chop us down to size, to lower the ceiling on our joy lest we be too happy?

Not at all. It is because of God's very desire that we be joyously happy, filled to overflowing with the uproarious cheer of heaven itself, that he says these things. For he is sending us down into honesty and sanity. He wants us to see our sickness so we can run to the doctor. He wants us to get healed.

Fallen human beings enter into joy only through the door of despair. Fullness can be had only through emptiness. That happens decisively at conversion, as we confess our hopelessly sinful predicament for the first time and collapse into the arms of Jesus, and then remains an ongoing rhythm throughout the Christian life. If you are not growing in Christ, one reason may be that you have drifted out of the salutary and healthy discipline of self-despair.

Martin Luther, as much as anyone in the history of the church, understood this. In *The Bondage of the Will* he wrote:

> God has assuredly promised his grace to the humble, that is, to those who lament and despair of themselves. But no man can be thoroughly humbled until he knows that his salvation is utterly beyond his own powers, devices, endeavors, will, and works, and depends entirely on the choice, will, and work of another, namely, of God alone. For as long as he is persuaded that he himself can do even the least thing toward his salvation, he retains some self-confidence and does not altogether despair of himself, and therefore he is not humbled before God, but presumes that there is—or at least hopes or desires that there may be—some place, time, and work for him, by which he may at length attain to salvation. But when a man has no doubt that everything depends on the will of God, then he completely despairs of himself and chooses nothing for himself, but waits for God to work; then he has come close to grace.[1]

1   Martin Luther, *The Bondage of the Will*, in *Career of the Reformer III*, in *Luther's Works*, ed. Jaroslav Pelikan and Helmut T. Lehmann, 55 vols. (Philadelphia: Fortress, 1955–1986), 33:61–62.

And Luther understood, as is evident throughout his writings, that this despair is not a one-time experience, only for conversion. Christian growth is, among other things, growth in sensing just how impoverished and powerless we are in our own strength—that is, just how hollow and futile our efforts to grow spiritually are on our own steam.

This chapter considers the healthy necessity of despairing of ourselves time and again if we are to get growing in our walk with Christ.

The Sinfulness of Sin

What is a human being's natural condition?

On the one hand, we are resplendent with glory. The image of God drenches us in glory and renders us utterly unlike any other creature in the universe. We build, we create art, we love, we work. We command this world. Which is as God intended. God put Adam in the garden of Eden "to work it and keep it" (Gen. 2:15). Those two Hebrew words denote cultivation and protection, respectively. And that's why every human being, made in the image of God, is on this planet. We were put here to develop this world, to conquer it, to master it.

But we are also ruined. The ancient rebellion of our Edenic grandparents flows down through every generation, its tragic repercussions infecting every aspect of our existence. Our bodies start powering down from about age thirty on. Disease and natural calamities sweep away large numbers of us in unpredictable horrors. And most insidious of all, our minds and hearts have been infected—we crave the forbidden, we celebrate others' misfortune, we hoard rather than give. In short, we construct our entire lives around the throne of Self. Romans 3 captures this in the way it speaks of sin infecting every part of the physical body (Rom. 3:9–18). Fallen humans are factories of filth.

At one level we who confess Christ quickly concede the reality of sin. But we profoundly underplay it. "Nobody's perfect," we acknowledge. "We all make mistakes." But the problem is not that we are going the right direction with occasional missteps. We are running the wrong direction. Evil is the ocean, not the islands, of our internal existence. "The hearts of the children of man are full of evil," the Bible says, "and madness is in their hearts while they live" (Eccles. 9:3).

The reality of this evil, what the Bible calls sin, is itself what prevents us from recognizing it. The old British preacher Martyn Lloyd-Jones explains: "You will never make yourself feel that you are a sinner, because there is a mechanism in you as a result of sin that will always be defending you against every accusation. We are all on very good terms with ourselves, and we can always put up a good case for ourselves."[2] It's like we have a disease, one symptom of which is that we feel healthy. This is why the Bible often speaks of our sinfulness as blindness (e.g., Isa. 6:10; 42:7; Matt. 15:14; 23:17; John 9:40–41; 2 Cor. 4:4; 1 John 2:11; Rev. 3:17).

And what I am trying to say is that the only sure foundation on which we can build spiritual growth is the solid ground of self-despair. To the degree that we minimize the evil within, we lower the ceiling on how deeply we can grow. We take a painkiller and go to sleep when we think we have a headache; we undergo chemotherapy when we know we have a brain tumor. The severity of our condition dictates the depth and seriousness of the medicine we know we need. If you view your sinfulness as a bothersome headache more than a lethal cancer, you will see tepid growth, if any. You won't see yourself as needing to grow all that much. But

---

2 Martyn Lloyd-Jones, *Seeking the Face of God: Nine Reflections on the Psalms* (Wheaton, IL: Crossway, 2005), 34.

when we see how desperately sick we are and how profoundly short we fall of the glory for which God intended us, we have already taken the first decisive step in bridging that vast gulf between who we are and who we were made to be. "Learn much of your own heart," wrote the Scottish pastor Robert Murray McCheyne, "and when you have learned all you can, remember you have seen but a few yards into a pit that is unfathomable."[3]

But we must understand our sinfulness in a comprehensive way. It is not only our immorality that reflects the evil within. Even our morality is shot through with evil. Does that seem unnecessarily dour and negative to you? Consider your own life. That act of service yesterday—was it in fact, at root, a matter of creating a perception of you and your virtue? Don't answer too quickly! The way you cheerfully greet those around you today—is it, upon further reflection, mainly fueled by what you want others to think of you? Is it not, as Augustine put it, vice clothed as virtue?[4]

New Testament letters such as 2 Peter and Jude were basically written to confront the evil of immorality. But letters such as Galatians and Colossians were written to confront the evil of false morality. We are so naturally wicked that we will bend anything into the service of Self. Indeed, throughout the four Gospels it is evident that morality, not immorality, is the greatest obstacle to fellowship with Jesus. The destitute and rejected were drawn to Jesus, wiping his feet with their hair and leaving all to be with him; the religious elite questioned and doubted and, ultimately, killed him.

3   Robert Murray McCheyne, in an 1840 letter, in Andrew A. Bonar, *Memoirs and Remains of the Rev. Robert Murray McCheyne* (Edinburgh: Oliphant, Anderson, and Ferrier, 1892), 293.
4   Saint Augustine, *City of God*, ed. Vernon J. Bourke, trans. Gerald G. Walsh, Demetrius B. Zema, Grace Monahan, and Daniel J. Honan (Garden City, NY: Image, 1958), 19.25.

Die before You Die

The point in all this is that we must come face-to-face with who we really are, left to our own steam. Christian salvation is not assistance. It is rescue. The gospel does not take our good and complete us with God's help; the gospel tells us we are dead and helpless, unable to contribute anything to our rescue but the sin that requires it. Christian salvation is not enhancing. It is resurrecting.

What we do at conversion, and what we continue to do ten thousand times thereafter, is not ask God to give our otherwise ordered lives a little boost from heaven. What we do is collapse. We let the despair about who we are, left to ourselves, wash over us. In short, we die. As a character rightly puts it in C. S. Lewis's *Till We Have Faces*: "Die before you die. There is no chance after."[5]

Despair is not an end in itself, of course. But it is a vital element of healthy spirituality. It cannot be bypassed. One reason some Christians remain shallow their whole lives is they do not allow themselves, ever more deeply throughout their lives, to pass through the painful corridor of honesty about who they really are. This was the mistake of the church at Laodicea. Jesus diagnosed their error: "You say, I am rich, I have prospered, and I need nothing, not realizing that you are wretched, pitiable, poor, blind, and naked" (Rev. 3:17).

We can make the same mistake today. So enter in to the joyous freefall of self-despair. I am not suggesting you downplay the glorious image of God that you are. I am suggesting you let yourself maintain throughout the whole course of your Christian journey a salutary remembrance of just how much evil resides within you, even as one born again. Feel your sinfulness. Let it humble you. Let it sober you.

---

5   C. S. Lewis, *Till We Have Faces: A Myth Retold* (New York: Harcourt, 1956), 279.

Beware of so filling your life with talk shows and phone calls that you don't regularly stop and consider the ruinous condition of your life apart from Christ. *You cannot feel the weight of your sinfulness strongly enough.* I never met a deep Christian who did not have a correspondingly deep sense of his or her own natural desolation.

The Supreme Contrast

We come face-to-face with our sinfulness not primarily by sitting and reflecting, looking within, pondering our hearts. We do need to do that; and in today's hyper-fast-paced world, too many of us never do stop and reflect on what is going on inside us. But self-reflection takes us only so far. The blackness within comes into clear focus only when we see it next to the white brightness of God himself. In his private notebook for theological reflection, Jonathan Edwards jotted down:

> If we could behold the infinite fountain of purity and holiness, and could see what an infinitely pure flame it is, and with what a pure brightness it shines, so that the heavens appear impure when compared with it; and then should behold some infinitely odious and detestable filthiness brought and set in its presence: would it not be natural to expect some ineffably vehement opposition made to it? and would not the want of it be indecent and shocking?[6]

We sense how desperate our plight is only when it is stacked up next to the infinite beauty of God himself. When an extraordinary catch of fish caused Peter to realize that the one in the boat with him was holy divinity embodied, he did not clap Jesus on the back and thank

---

6 Jonathan Edwards, "Miscellany 779," in *The Works of Jonathan Edwards*, vol. 18, *The "Miscellanies," 501–832*, ed. Ava Chamberlain (New Haven, CT: Yale University Press, 2000), 438.

him for a good day's catch. He fell down on his face. Peter's words are arresting: "Depart from me, for I am a sinful man" (Luke 5:8).

Have you experienced this? Do you know what it is to see yourself as vile and vulnerable in the presence of Fullness himself?

We will not grow, not deeply anyway, except by going through the painful death of being honest about our own spiritual bankruptcy. We must see and feel our utter emptiness and innate rebellion and resistance in the presence of a God whose infinitude of beauty and perfection exposes such sinfulness.

The Great Prerequisite

If you feel stuck, defeated by old sin patterns, leverage that despair into the healthy sense of self-futility that is the door through which you must pass if you are to get real spiritual traction. Let your emptiness humble you. Let it take you *down*. Not to stay there, wallowing, but to shed the facile optimism that we so naturally believe of ourselves.

We will come to the positive counterparts to this death in chapters ahead. But we cannot circumvent this stage. It is the great prerequisite to everything else. The pattern of the Christian life is not a straight line up to resurrection existence but a curve down into death and thereby up into resurrection existence.[7] And one thing that means is that we go through life with an ever-deepening sense of how reprehensible, in ourselves, we really are. It was toward the *end* of his life that Paul identified himself as the most award-winning sinner he knew (1 Tim. 1:15). The godliest octogenarians I know are those who feel themselves to be more sinful now than at any time before. They

---

7 See Paul E. Miller, *J-Curve: Dying and Rising with Jesus in Everyday Life* (Wheaton, IL: Crossway, 2019).

have known the pattern of healthy self-despair. Who of us cannot relate to what the pastor and hymn-writer John Newton wrote in a 1776 letter (at age fifty-one): "The life of faith seems so simple and easy in theory, that I can point it out to others in few words; but in practice it is very difficult, and my advances are so slow, that I hardly dare say I get forward at all."[8]

Have you been brought to despair of what you can achieve in your sanctification? If not, have the courage to look yourself squarely in the mirror. Repent. See your profound poverty. Ask the Lord to forgive your arrogance. As you descend down into death, into knowledge of the futility of what inner change you can achieve by your own efforts, it is there, right there, in that dismay and emptiness, *that God lives.* It is there in that desert that he loves to cause the waters to flow and the trees to bloom. Your despair is all he needs to work with. "Only acknowledge your guilt" (Jer. 3:13). What will ruin your growth is if you look the other way, if you deflect the searching gaze of Purity himself, if you cover over your sinfulness and emptiness with smiles and jokes and then go check your mutual funds again, holding at bay what you know in your deepest heart: you are wicked.

If you plunge down only a little into self-despair, you will rise only a little into joyous growth in Christ. "The index of the soundness of a man's faith in Christ," writes J. I. Packer, "is the genuineness of the self-despair from which it springs."[9] Don't just admit your condition is desperately ruinous. Let yourself feel it. Ponder, unhurriedly, how vile, left to yourself, you are.

---

8 *Letters of John Newton* (Edinburgh: Banner of Truth, 2007), 184; similarly 212–13, and indeed this is a repeated theme throughout Newton's letters.
9 J. I. Packer, *A Quest for Godliness: The Puritan Vision of the Christian Life* (1990; repr., Wheaton, IL: Crossway, 2010), 170.

Newton captured precisely the way real growth comes only *through* (not by skipping) despair in his 1779 hymn "I Asked the Lord That I Might Grow":

> I asked the Lord that I might grow
> In faith, and love, and every grace;
> Might more of His salvation know,
> And seek, more earnestly, His face.
>
> 'Twas He who taught me thus to pray,
> And He, I trust, has answered prayer!
> But it has been in such a way,
> As almost drove me to despair.
>
> I hoped that in some favored hour,
> At once He'd answer my request;
> And by His love's constraining pow'r,
> Subdue my sins, and give me rest.
>
> Instead of this, He made me feel
> The hidden evils of my heart;
> And let the angry pow'rs of hell
> Assault my soul in every part.
>
> Yea more, with His own hand He seemed
> Intent to aggravate my woe;
> Crossed all the fair designs I schemed,
> Blasted my gourds, and laid me low.
>
> Lord, why is this, I trembling cried,
> Wilt thou pursue thy worm to death?
> "'Tis in this way," the Lord replied,
> "I answer prayer for grace and faith.

"These inward trials I employ,
From self, and pride, to set thee free;
And break thy schemes of earthly joy,
That thou may'st find thy all in Me."

Pave the way for real growth in Christ through deep, honest, healthy despair.

Collapse

But once we have despaired of our own capacities to generate growth—what then? And time and again throughout our lives—even today, as we come to grips yet again with our sinfulness—what do we do?

There is nothing noble about staying in that pit of despair. We need to experience it. But we are not meant to dwell in it. Healthy despair is an intersection, not a highway; a gateway, not a pathway. We must go there. But we dare not stay there.

The Bible teaches, rather, that each experience of despair is to melt us afresh into deeper fellowship with Jesus. Like jumping on a trampoline, we are to go down into freshly felt emptiness but then let that spring us high into fresh heights with Jesus. The Bible calls this two-step movement repentance and faith.

Repentance is turning from Self. Faith is turning to Jesus. You can't have one without the other. Repentance that does not turn to Jesus is not real repentance; faith that has not first turned from Self is not real faith. If we are traveling the wrong direction, things get fixed as we turn away from the wrong direction and simultaneously begin going the right direction. Both happen together.

Some Christians seem to think that the Christian life is ignited with a decisive act of repentance and then fed by faith thereafter. But as Luther taught, all of life is repentance. The first thesis of his

Ninety-Five Theses reads, "When our Lord and Master Jesus Christ said, 'Repent' (Matt. 4:17), he willed the entire life of believers to be one of repentance." The Christian life is one of *repenting our way forward.*

Equally, we live our whole lives by faith. Paul said not "I was converted by faith" but "I live by faith" (Gal. 2:20). We do not merely begin the Christian life by faith; we progress by faith. It is our new normal. We process life, we navigate this mortal existence, by a moment-by-moment turning to God in trust and hope at each juncture, each decision, each passing hour. We "walk by faith, not by sight" (2 Cor. 5:7). That is, we move through life with our eyes looking ever up. Our posture is one of expectant empowering from above.

Repentance and faith. In a word: collapse.

Both repentance and faith, however, must never be viewed in isolation from Jesus himself. They are connectors to Christ. They are not "our contribution." They simply are the roads by which we get to real healing: Christ himself. As Jack Miller wisely put it in a 1983 letter to a young friend:

> When you turn to Christ, you don't have a repentance apart from Christ, you just have Christ. Therefore don't seek repentance or faith as such but seek Christ. When you have Christ you have repentance and faith. Beware of seeking an experience of repentance; just seek an experience of Christ.
>
> The Devil can be pretty tricky. He doesn't mind you thinking much about repentance and faith if you do not think about Jesus Christ. . . . Seek Christ, and relate to Christ as a loving Savior and Lord who wants to invite you to know him.[10]

---

10 In Barbara Miller Juliani, *The Heart of a Servant Leader: Letters from Jack Miller* (Phillipsburg, NJ: P&R, 2004), 244–45.

As you despair of yourself—agonizing over the desolation wrought by your failures, your weaknesses, your inadequacies—let that despair take you way down deep into honesty with yourself. For there you will find a friend, the living Lord Jesus himself, who will startle and surprise you with his gentle goodness as you leave Self behind, in repentance, and bank on him afresh, in faith.

3

Union

WE HAVE SHARPENED OUR VISION of who Jesus is. And we have established the ongoing salutary reality of self-despair and collapsing in penitent faith time and again into the arms of that Jesus. But does this Jesus remain at a distance? How do we actually access him? What is the nature of our relationship with him?

The New Testament gives a resounding answer. Those who collapse into him in repentance and faith are united to him—joined to him—*one* with him. This, and not the doctrine of justification or reconciliation or adoption or any other important biblical teaching—is the controlling center, according to the New Testament, of what it means to be a Christian. The New Testament refers to our being united to Christ over two hundred times. That averages out to about one reference per page in many Bible layouts. If a book loops back to the same theme on every page, wouldn't you consider it a major point the author intends to get across?

But what does this have to do with our spiritual growth? Everything. The old writer Jeremiah Burroughs put it this way: "From Christ as from a fountain sanctification flows into the souls of the saints: their sanctification comes not so much from their struggling, and endeavors, and vows, and resolutions, as it comes flowing to them from their union with him."[1] But don't take it from the Puritans. The doctrine of union with Christ is where the Bible itself goes when tackling the question of how believers grow In Romans 6, Paul addresses the objection of why the gospel of grace is not an encouragement to sin all the more by bringing in the reality of a believer's union with Christ:

> Are we to continue in sin that grace may abound? By no means! How can we who died to sin still live in it? Do you not know that all of us who have been baptized into Christ Jesus were baptized into his death? We were buried therefore with him by baptism into death, in order that, just as Christ was raised from the dead by the glory of the Father, we too might walk in newness of life. For if we have been united with him in a death like his, we shall certainly be united with him in a resurrection like his. (Rom. 6:1–5)

The logic of the text is this: yes, more sin means more grace, and his grace always outstrips our sinning; but believers do not therefore sin it up all the more, because his grace is not a transaction; rather, his grace comes to us through union. When Jesus went down into the grave to die *for* our sins, we too went with him down into that grave to die *to* our sins. What would we say to an adopted orphan wandering out the front door of the mansion of his new family and down to the food stamps line? We'd say: *What are you doing? That's not who you are anymore.* We find similar logic in books of the New Testament such as Ephesians and Colossians.

In this chapter we'll consider exactly what union with Christ is and how this doctrine nurtures spiritual growth.

---

1   Quoted in Ernest F. Kevan, *The Grace of Law: A Study in Puritan Theology* (Grand Rapids, MI: Reformation Heritage, 1997), 236.

God in Me

There are basically four different ways Christians understand growth.[2] The first three are more or less common in different parts of the church. The fourth is what the Bible gives us. We'll call these

1. God then me,
2. God not me,
3. God plus me,
4. God in me.

A "God then me" mindset, first, believes it is God who does everything to save me—he opens my eyes, he regenerates me, he grants me new life—and he gives me a fresh start at life, a blank slate. So then it's up to me to get busy serving him, showing him how grateful I am for all he has done. Faith alone gets me in, then effort is what moves me along. After all, this way of thinking goes, we've been indwelt by the Spirit, so we should be living radically transformed lives. The trouble with this approach is that it does not account for the ongoing presence of sin in the life of the believer. Nor does it allow for the pervasive biblical theme of the ongoing grace and mercy of God in the life of the believer, which we'll dwell on in a later chapter.

Others, second, understand growth as "God not me." This is essentially the polar opposite of the first error. The idea here is that God saves me, and then the Christian life is a matter of God, and only God, bringing any growth in my life. It's a "let go and let God" mindset that treats our human agency as passive, as if we can only

2   I picked up this fourfold taxonomy from Jerry Bridges at some point, though I do not remember where.

wait for God to act upon us. While the previous mindset was too optimistic about what believers are capable of in their own strength, this one is too pessimistic about what they can do in Christ. While the previous error emphasized human responsibility in sanctification to the neglect of divine sovereignty, this one emphasizes divine sovereignty to the neglect of human responsibility. But Scripture speaks of sanctification as a matter of both divine sovereignty and human responsibility.

We're calling the third approach "God plus me." This one is getting closer to the truth. The idea here is that Christian growth is a collaborative effort. God does some; I do some. We are partners. Each party contributes something. If we picture each growth approach as a circle, the "God then me" approach has the circle entirely filled up with me, the "God not me" circle is filled entirely with God, and the "God plus me" circle has a squiggly line down the middle, with roughly one half filled with God and the other half filled with me.

But the proper approach would have both God and me entirely filling the circle. The two agents are overlaid. This fourth approach is "God *in* me." God does everything to save me, and then by his Holy Spirit (more on that in another chapter) he *unites* me spiritually to his Son. The result is that in our growth in holiness (as Edwards put it) "we are not merely passive in it, nor yet does God do some and we do the rest, but God does all, and we do all. . . . We are in different respects wholly passive and wholly active."[3] This approach, in other words, holds together both human responsibility and divine sovereignty in how we move forward spiritually.

---

3   Jonathan Edwards, "Efficacious Grace," in *The Works of Jonathan Edwards*, vol. 21, *Writings on the Trinity, Grace, and Faith*, ed. Sang Hyun Lee (New Haven, CT: Yale University Press, 2003), 251.

The Biblical Evidence

Consider how the Bible speaks about our spiritual vitality. Notice the way God is always held up as the one supremely responsible for our growth, yet never in a way that cancels out our own efforts.

> But by the grace of God I am what I am, and his grace toward[4] me was not in vain. On the contrary, I worked harder than any of them, though it was not I, but the grace of God that is with me. (1 Cor. 15:10)

> Therefore, my beloved, as you have always obeyed, so now, not only as in my presence but much more in my absence, work out your own salvation with fear and trembling, for it is God who works in you, both to will and to work for his good pleasure. (Phil. 2:12–13)

> For this I toil, struggling with all his energy that he powerfully works within me. (Col. 1:29)

Your Christian growth is a matter of divine grace. You cannot crowbar yourself into growth. You must be lifted into growth. But the divine grace that brings about change is a divine grace that fuels and fills our own efforts. For we are *in* the Son.

Safe and Secure

But what does this mean? What is it to be united to Christ? Admittedly, it is an elusive concept. We can picture a baby kangaroo being "in" its mother's pouch. But in what sense are we "in" Christ?

The first thing to note is simply the sheer intimacy and safety of being a Christian. Our Christian growth takes place in the sphere

---

4   This could equally be translated "his grace *in* me."

of a wonderful inevitability, even invincibility. I am united to Christ. I can never be disunited from him. The logic of the New Testament letters is that in order for me to get disunited from Christ, Christ himself would have to be de-resurrected. He'd have to get kicked out of heaven for me to get kicked out of him. We're that safe.

The Scottish pastor and theologian James Stewart (1896–1990) rightly understood the centrality of the doctrine of union with Christ and explained it vividly:

> Christ is the redeemed man's new environment. He has been lifted out of the cramping restrictions of his earthly lot into a totally different sphere, the sphere of Christ. He has been transplanted into a new soil and a new climate, and both soil and climate are Christ. His spirit is breathing a nobler element. He is moving on a loftier plane.[5]

If you can bear with an irreverent illustration, think of yourself as an onion. The outer peel consists of the peripheral things about you, the parts of you that don't matter much: your clothes, the car you drive, things like that. If you peel away that layer, what's next? A collection of things slightly more essential to who you are: the family you were raised in, your personality profile, your blood type, your volunteer work. Peel that away. The next deeper layer is your relationships: your dearest friends, your roommates if you're a student, your spouse if you're married. Peel that away. The next deeper layer is what you believe about the world, the truths you cherish deep in your heart: who you believe God is, what your final future is, where you think world history is heading. The next deeper layer after that

---

5 James S. Stewart, *A Man in Christ: The Vital Elements of St. Paul's Religion* (London: Hodder and Stoughton, 1935), 157.

comprises your sins and secrets, past and present, things about you no one else knows.

Keep peeling away layer after layer, everything that makes you *you*. What do you find at the core? You are united to Christ. That is the most irreducible reality about you. Peel everything else away, and the solid, immovable truth about you is your union with a resurrected Christ.

How could it be otherwise? After all, you did not engineer your union with Christ yourself. We read in 2 Timothy 1:8–9 of "God, who saved us and called us to a holy calling, not because of our works but because of his own purpose and grace, which he gave us *in Christ Jesus* before the ages began." We didn't wake up one morning and go online to unionwithchrist.com and click yes. What is most deeply true of us is that we were secured *in* Christ before we had ever heard *of* Christ. Only in the relaxed safety of your eternally secured union with Christ can true growth blossom.

The Macro Dimension

But we're still left wondering what union with Christ *means*. And the answer to that is that the New Testament uses the language of union with Christ in basically two ways.[6] We could call them the macro and the micro realities to union with Christ, or the cosmic and the intimate, or the federal and the personal.

The macro dimension to union with Christ is that he is your leader, and as he goes, so you go. His fate is yours. Why? Because you are in

---

6　For a technical and rigorous book-length treatment, specifically focusing on Paul's letters, see Constantine R. Campbell, *Paul and Union with Christ: An Exegetical and Theological Study* (Grand Rapids, MI: Zondervan, 2015), which speaks of four meanings to the New Testament language of union with Christ.

him. That may sound a little odd, especially for those of us who live in the West today. But for most human cultures throughout most of human history, including Bible times, this way of thinking about a leader and his people was normal and natural. The formal name for it is "corporate solidarity." If you've ever heard Christ referred to as believers' "federal" head, that's getting at the same notion. The idea is that the one represents the many, and the many are represented by the one.

We see it, for example, in 2 Corinthians 5:14, speaking of the work of Christ and how it connects to us: "One has died for all, therefore all have died." Because Christ died, and those united to him share in his fate, we too have "died." We see the same logic in Romans 6: "We know that our old self was crucified with him. . . . We have died with Christ" (vv. 6, 8).

To be in Christ, then, in this macro or cosmic or federal way, is for our destiny to be bound up with his rather than with Adam's. First Corinthians 15:22 is the whole Bible in a short sentence: "As in Adam all die, so also in Christ shall all be made alive." The alternative to being in Christ is to be in Adam. One or the other. No third option. Every human being alive today is either in Adam or in Christ. And that is the fundamental defining reality about each of us. The most famous athletes, the cultural icons, those whose fans treat them like gods—what is most deeply true of them is that they are either in Adam or in Christ.

We can be even more specific. The message of the New Testament is absolutely thrilling at this point and deeply fosters our growth. In being transferred from the destiny of Adam to the destiny of Christ, we are transferred not simply from one *person* to another but from one *aeon* to another. When Jesus Christ rose from the dead, the new age that the Old Testament had long anticipated quietly erupted on the scene of human history. To be united to Christ as your new federal head is to be placed in that new realm. If you are a Christian, you have been swept up by divine grace into the new order that the prophets foretold. The new creation has already begun to dawn. It often doesn't feel like it, because the old fallen age continues steamrolling right alongside the dawning new age. We remain fallen sinners. But our basic identity, our fundamental location, is in the new age, because we are in Christ. Christ plunged through death and out the other side into the dawning new creation, and to be "in" him means that he has pulled you with him. To render 2 Corinthians 5:17 woodenly, "If anyone is in Christ—new creation." In the Greek text there is no verb. What Paul is saying is that if you are in Christ, you have been swept up into Eden 2.0, the new creation that silently erupted when Christ walked out of that tomb.

As you consider your own messy little life, therefore, consider who you are. Consider whose you are. Consider that Christ's resurrection is the guarantee that you too will be raised one day physically. Consider that you have already been raised spiritually (Eph. 2:6; Col. 2:12; 3:1). When you sin, you behave out of accord with who you now are. You're acting like a former orphan who's been adopted yet keeps running out of his new house to the curb to beg for bread when the kitchen is fully stocked and freely his. You are destined for glory.

The Micro Dimension

But there is a closer, more intimate reality to union with Christ, and sometimes the biblical authors speak of our union in this way. It is difficult to know exactly how to express it. The Bible uses imagery to communicate it, perhaps because this reality is better likened than defined. We are given images such as a vine and its branches, or a head and the other body parts, or even a groom and his bride. In all cases there is an organic, intimate uniting, a sharing of properties, a oneness. The vine gives life to the branches; the head directs and cares for its body parts; the husband "nourishes and cherishes" his wife as he does his own body (Eph. 5:29).

One passage is particularly arresting. Consider what Paul is saying about our union with Christ in 1 Corinthians 6 as he encourages us toward sexual purity:

> The body is not meant for sexual immorality, but for the Lord, and the Lord for the body. And God raised the Lord and will also raise us up by his power. Do you not know that your bodies are members of Christ? Shall I then take the members of Christ and make them members of a prostitute? Never! Or do you not know that he who is joined to a prostitute becomes one body with her? For, as it is written, "The two will become one flesh." But he who is joined to the Lord becomes one spirit with him. Flee from sexual immorality. (1 Cor. 6:13–18)

"The Lord" here refers to Jesus, and "members" means body parts. Do you follow the logic of what Paul is saying? His point is that we are so *one* with Christ that to be united to a prostitute is to unite Christ with a prostitute. I say it cautiously, and with reverence, but I must ask you what the text is insisting on: Do you want to be responsible for Jesus committing fornication? For you to commit sexual immorality is—by virtue of your union with Christ—to cause Christ, in some sense, to do so likewise. I do not mean that we can actually make the risen Christ sin in that way. I am simply noticing what the text says—"Shall I then take the members of Christ and make them members of a prostitute?"—and observing how vital and powerful and intimate a thing our union with the Lord Jesus must be for Paul to say what he says here.

Your salvation in the gospel is far deeper, far more wondrous, than walking an aisle or praying a prayer or raising a hand or going forward at an evangelistic rally. Your salvation is to be united to the living Christ himself. It is, as Scougal wrote, "a union of the soul with God, a real participation of the divine nature."[7]

Perhaps this creates a problem in your mind. If every Christian is united to the same Christ, what happens to our individuality? Will we all begin to look more and more like one another, losing our distinctive individual personhood? The answer is that at one level, yes, we will all begin to look more like Christ and thus more like one another—each of us exhibiting more love, joy, peace, patience, kindness, goodness, faithfulness, gentleness, and self-control (Gal. 5:22–23).

But in terms of our individual distinctiveness, the glory of Christian redemption is that it is in union with Jesus that we are given back our true selves. We finally begin becoming who we were truly created to be. C. S. Lewis offers a brilliant analogy to make the point.[8] If a group of people have always lived in the dark and are told a light is going to be turned on so that they will all be able to see each other, they may very well object, believing that since a single lamp will be shining the same light on everyone, they will all look identical to each other. But, of course, we know that the light would bring out their individual distinctiveness. Union with a single Christ is like that. You are given back your true self. You become the you that you were

---

7   Henry Scougal, *The Life of God in the Soul of Man* (Fearn, Ross-shire, Scotland: Christian Focus, 1996), 41–42.

8   C. S. Lewis, *Mere Christianity* (1952; repr., New York: Touchstone, 1996), 189.

meant to be. You recover your original destiny. You realize that your existence out of Christ was a shadow of what you were made to be. Your distinctive personality, your *you*-ness, your human individuality, was in 2D when you were out of Christ, held back by sin and shame and fear and darkness. Now that you are in Christ, you are in 3D, free to blossom. In other words, it is only in union with Christ that you can grow into who God made you to be.

The Umbrella Doctrine

At this point you may be wondering how union with Christ fits with the other great and glorious pictures of our salvation—justification, adoption, and so on. The answer is that union with Christ is the umbrella doctrine within which every benefit of salvation is subsumed. When we are united to Christ, we get all these benefits. John Calvin began his discussion of salvation in the *Institutes* by saying, "We must understand that as long as Christ remains outside of us, and we are separated from him, all that he has suffered and done for the salvation of the human race remains useless."[9]

Ponder the rich variety of ways the New Testament speaks of our rescue in Christ. With each I've identified two texts that teach that aspect of salvation, and then given in parentheses that blessing's opposite (what that aspect of salvation delivers us *from*).

- Justification—the *law-court* metaphor (Rom. 5:1; Titus 3:7) (no longer condemned)
- Sanctification—the *cultic* metaphor (1 Cor. 1:2; 1 Thess. 4:3) (no longer defiled)

---

9 John Calvin, *Institutes of the Christian Religion*, ed. John T. McNeill, trans. Ford Lewis Battles (Louisville: Westminster John Knox, 1960), 3.1.1.

- Adoption—the *familial* metaphor (Rom. 8:15; 1 John 3:1–2) (no longer orphaned)
- Reconciliation—the *relational* metaphor (Rom. 5:1–11; 2 Cor. 5:18–20) (no longer estranged)
- Washing—the *physical-cleansing* metaphor (1 Cor. 6:11; Titus 3:5) (no longer dirty)
- Redemption—the *slave-market* metaphor (Eph. 1:7; Rev. 14:3–4) (no longer enslaved)
- Purchase—the *financial* metaphor (1 Cor. 6:20; 2 Pet. 2:1) (no longer in debt)
- Liberation—the *imprisonment* metaphor (Gal. 5:1; Rev. 1:5) (no longer imprisoned)
- New birth—the *physical-generation* metaphor (John 3:3–7; 1 Pet. 1:3, 23) (no longer nonexistent)
- Illumination—the *light* metaphor (John 12:35–36; 2 Cor. 4:4–6) (no longer blind)
- Resurrection—the *bodily* metaphor (Eph. 2:6; Col. 3:1) (no longer dead)

And union with Christ, the *organic* or *spatial* metaphor, is the master-picture. If you are in Christ, you get all these benefits. It's all or nothing. This is why Paul says that because of God's saving work "you are in Christ Jesus, who became to us wisdom from God, righteousness and sanctification and redemption" (1 Cor. 1:30).[10] The point is that he's the total-package, high-octane, no-weaknesses

---

10 Even justification, which in the evangelical world tends to be centralized above other saving realities, takes place only in Christ. "For our sake [God] made him to be sin who knew no sin, so that *in him* we might become the righteousness of God" (2 Cor. 5:21). Elsewhere Paul speaks of wanting to "gain Christ and be found *in him*, not having a righteousness of my own" (Phil. 3:8–9). In both these texts the noun "righteousness" is the same root used to speak of justification.

Savior. All you need to do is get into him, which happens irreversibly at conversion by yielding, surrendering, trusting faith.[11]

Taking It Deep

We've been working hard in this chapter to get clear on what the Bible teaches about union with Christ. But the whole point of understanding clearly the truths of the Bible is so that our comfort and joy soar as we melt into calmed reassurance of who God actually is and who we are.

As we begin to wind down this chapter on union with Christ, I want to ask you to let your mind and heart go way down deep into the reality of this truth. Remember, the point of this book is that Christian growth is an enterprise not mainly in adding but in deepening. If you are in Christ, you have everything you need to grow. You are united to Christ: by the Holy Spirit, you are in him and he is in you. He is your federal head, and he is your intimate companion. *You cannot lose.* You are inexhaustibly rich. For you are one with Christ, and he is himself inexhaustibly rich, the heir of the universe. Jonathan Edwards spoke of union with Christ like this:

> By virtue of the believer's union with Christ, he does in fact possess all things. But it may be asked, how does he possess all things? What is he the better for it? How is a true Christian so much richer than other people?
>
> To answer this, I'll tell you what I mean by "possessing all things." I mean that God three in one, all that he is, and all that he has, and

---

11 The German New Testament scholar Adolf Deissmann discovered and showed, in a seminal study, that the most distinctive element of New Testament Christianity is that of the union of the adherent to the God he worships (Deissmann, *Die neutestamentliche Formel "in Christo Jesu"* [Marburg: Elwert, 1892]).

all that he does, all that he has made or done—the whole universe, bodies and spirits, earth and heaven, angels, humans and devils, sun, moon and stars, land and sea, fish and fowls, all silver and gold, kings and potentates—are as much the Christian's as the money in his pocket, the clothes he wears, the house he dwells in, or the victuals he eats; yes, properly his, advantageously his, by virtue of the union with Christ; because Christ, who certainly does possess all things, is entirely his: so that the Christian possesses it all, more than a wife the share of the best and dearest husband, more than the hand possesses what the head does. It is all his.

Every atom in the universe is managed by Christ so as to be most to the advantage of the Christian, every particle of air or every ray of the sun; so that he in the other world, when he comes to see it, shall sit and enjoy all this vast inheritance with surprising, amazing joy.[12]

Why is that true for any of us? Only, Edwards says, because we are united to Christ.

Submerge yourself in this truth. Let it wash over you. The divine Son, through whom all things were made (Col. 1:16), who "upholds the universe by the word of his power" (Heb. 1:3), the one without whose constant care and guidance all of molecular reality would fall apart (Col. 1:17), is the one with whom you have been united. Through no activity of your own, but by the sheer and mighty grace of God, you have been enveloped in the triumphant and tender ruler of the cosmos.

---

12 Jonathan Edwards, "Miscellany ff," in *The Works of Jonathan Edwards*, vol. 13, *The "Miscellanies,"* *a–500*, ed. Thomas A. Schafer (New Haven, CT: Yale University Press, 1994), 183; language slightly updated.

Therefore: *nothing can touch you that does not touch him.* To get to you, every pain, every assault, every disappointment has to go through him. You are shielded by invincible love. Everything that washes into your life, no matter how hard, comes from and through the tender care of the friend of sinners. He himself feels your anguish even more deeply than you do, because you're one with him; and he mediates everything hard in your life through his love for you, because you're one with him. Picture yourself standing in a circle with an invisible but impenetrable wall surrounding you, a sphere of impregnability. But it's not a circle you're in. It's a person—*the* person. The one before whom John fell down as he grappled for words to describe what he was looking at as one whose "eyes were like a flame of fire . . . and his voice was like the roar of many waters" (Rev. 1:14–15) has been made one with you. The might of heaven, the power that flung galaxies into existence, has swept you into himself.

And you're there to stay. Amid the storms of your little existence— the sins and sufferings, the failure and faltering, the waywardness and wandering—he is going to walk you right into heaven. He is not just with you. He is in you, and you in him. His destiny now falls on you. His union with you at both the macro and micro levels guarantees your eventual glory and rest and calm. You may as well question gravity as question the certainty of what your union with him means for your final future.

So consider the darkness that remains in your life. The spiritual lethargy. The habitual sin. The deep-seated resentment. That place in your life where you feel most defeated. Our sins loom large. They seem so insurmountable. But Christ and your union with him loom larger still. As far as sin in your life reaches, Christ and your union with him reach further. As deep as your failure goes, Christ and your union with him go deeper still. As strong as your sin feels, the bond of your oneness with Jesus Christ is stronger still. Live the rest of your life mindful of your union with the prince of heaven. Rest in the knowledge that your sins and failures can never kick you out of Christ. Let an ever-deepening awareness of your union with him strengthen your resistance to sin. See it in the Bible. Ponder his tireless care for you. You have been strengthened with the power to fight and overcome sin because the power that raised Jesus from the dead now resides in you, living and active—for Jesus Christ himself resides in you. You can never be justifiably accused ever again. "There is therefore now no condemnation for those who are *in* Christ Jesus" (Rom. 8:1).

Draw strength from your oneness with Jesus. You are no longer alone. No longer isolated. When you sin, don't give up. Let him pick you up and put you on your feet again with fresh dignity. He lifts your chin, looks you in the eye, and defines your existence: "you in me, and I in you" (John 14:20).

4

Embrace

THE FIRST THREE CHAPTERS have primarily been laying the foundation—Jesus Christ's fullness (chap. 1), our emptiness (chap. 2), and our union with him (chap. 3). Now we begin to get into the actual dynamics by which believers change. We begin with the love of God.

My first challenge is not, however, to convince you that God loves you. You know that. You cannot be a Christian without knowing it. My first challenge is to convince you of how much greater God's love is than even now you conceive. At the end of the book of Job, Job said,

> I had heard of you by the hearing of the ear,
> but now my eye sees you. (42:5)

That experience is what many of us need to step into in order to get growing again in our Christian lives. If you are stalled out, if your discipleship is not merely marked by occasional stumbling but defined by it, you need what Job experienced. You have heard of divine love. But now you need to see it. And spend a lifetime seeing it ever more deeply, ever more expansively. Your vision of the love of God needs to be not just heard but seen; not just known but tasted.

What is the love of God? To ask that question is the same as to ask, what is God? The Bible says not simply that "God loves" but also that "God is love" (1 John 4:8, 16). Love, for the God of the Bible, is not one activity among others. Love defines who he is most deeply. Ultimate reality is not cold, blank, endless space. Ultimate reality is an eternal fountain of endless, unquenchable love. A love so great and so free that it could not be contained within the uproarious joy of Father, Son, and Spirit but spilled out to create and embrace finite and fallen humans into it. Divine love is inherently spreading, engulfing, embracing, overflowing. If you are a Christian, *God made you so that he could love you.* His embrace of you is the point of your life. I know you don't feel it. Even that is taken care of. He wants you to know a love that is yours even when you feel undeserving or numb.

What I want to say in this chapter is that the love of God is not something to see once and believe and then move beyond to other truths or strategies for growing in Christ. The love of God is what we feed on our whole lives long, wading ever more deeply into this endless ocean. And that feeding, that wading, is itself what fosters growth. *We grow in Christ no further than we enjoy his embrace of us.* His tender, mighty, irreversible embrace into his own divine heart.

Perhaps no passage takes us into the endless love of God for messy sinners as deeply as the end of Ephesians 3. Let Ephesians 3 be a strong and gentle friend who leads you by the hand into the most stable reality at the heart of the universe: the love of God and of Christ.

The Unknowable Love of Christ

Paul didn't pray the tepid prayers we often pray. He prayed God-sized prayers. In one of the most spiritually nuclear passages in all the Bible he prays to the Father that according to the riches of his glory he may grant you to be strengthened with power through his Spirit in your inner being, so that Christ may dwell in your hearts through faith—that you, being rooted and grounded in love, may have strength to comprehend with all the saints what is the breadth and length and height and depth, and to know the love of Christ that surpasses knowledge, that you may be filled with all the fullness of God. (Eph. 3:16–19)

If we were to pray that reality into our lives and into our churches, what story would we be telling from heaven?

What exactly is Paul praying for? Not for greater obedience among the Ephesians, or that they would be more fruitful, or that false teaching would be stamped out, or that they would grow in doctrinal depth, or even for the spread of the gospel. All good things, things we should and must pray for. But here Paul prays that the Ephesians would be given supernatural power—not power to perform miracles or walk on water or convert their neighbors, but power, such power, the kind that only God himself can give, power to *know how much Jesus loves them*. Not just to have the love of Christ. To *know* the love of Christ.

What's the state of your soul today, as you read this book? Consider your own inner life. Ponder Christ. Do you know the love of Christ? Remember, Paul wrote Ephesians to a church. He was writing to believers, to people who had already come to terms, once and for all at the point of conversion, with the love of Jesus for them. Yet Paul prays that they would know the love of Christ. Apparently, there's knowing the love of Christ, and there's knowing the love of Christ. Verse 19 literally reads "to know the surpassing-knowledge love of Christ." Paul is praying that they would know what cannot be known. Remember, "knowing" in the Bible is not merely cognitive.

It is profoundly relational. Even sexual intimacy is described as a man "knowing" his wife. As Jonathan Edwards famously put it, you can "know" honey in two distinct ways: you can know the exact chemical makeup of honey; or you can taste it. Both are ways we can "know" honey. But only the latter is the knowledge by which honey is experienced.[1]

And here in Ephesians 3, Paul is praying that believers would taste the love of Christ. Drink it down. Like Job's vision of God, what Paul prays for is that our apprehension of the love of Christ would go from audio to video. It's the difference between looking at a postcard of the Hawaii beach and sitting on that beach, blinking, squinting, absorbing the sun's warmth.

Unflappable Affection

What is this love of Christ?

Niceness? Certainly not—this is the Christ who took the time to make a whip and then used it to drive the money changers from the temple, flipping over tables.

Is it a refusal to judge people? By no means: Scripture speaks of his judgment like a sharp two-edged sword coming out of his mouth (Rev. 1:16; 2:12).

The love of Christ is his settled, unflappable heart of affection for sinners and sufferers—and *only* sinners and sufferers. When Jesus loves, Jesus is Jesus. He is being true to his own innermost depths. He doesn't have to work himself up to love. He is a gorged river of love, pent up, ready to gush forth upon the most timid request for it.

---

1   Jonathan Edwards, "A Divine and Supernatural Light," in *The Works of Jonathan Edwards*, vol. 17, *Sermons and Discourses, 1730–1733*, ed. Mark Valeri (New Haven, CT: Yale University Press, 1999), 414.

Love is who Jesus most deeply, most naturally is. The Puritan John Bunyan put it this way in speaking of Christ's love: "Love in him is essential to his being. God is love; Christ is God; therefore Christ is love, *love naturally*. He may as well cease to be, as cease to love."[2]

Notice what the text of Ephesians 3 says. Paul wants believers "to comprehend the breadth and length and height and depth" (v. 18)—but of what? It's not immediately obvious. What we do see, though, is that he then goes on immediately to say he wants them "to know the love of Christ" (v. 19). There is a parallel between "to comprehend" and "to know":

- "to comprehend . . . what is the breadth and length and height and depth" (v. 18)
- "to know the love of Christ that surpasses knowledge" (v. 19)

This parallel leads us to conclude that it is Christ's love itself that is expansive in its "breadth and length and height and depth." This is striking because only one other reality in the universe is boundless, endless, without limits—God himself.

Paul is saying that the love of Christ is as expansive as God himself. We can underestimate it. We always do. We can never overestimate it. "His essence being love," Jonathan Edwards preached, "he is as it were an infinite ocean of love without shores and bottom, yea, and without a surface."[3] The love of Christ is a love next to which every human romance is the faintest whisper.

2 John Bunyan, *The Saints' Knowledge of the Love of Christ*, in *The Works of John Bunyan*, ed. George Offer, 3 vols. (repr., Edinburgh: Banner of Truth, 1991), 2:17; emphasis original.
3 Jonathan Edwards, "The Terms of Prayer," in *The Works of Jonathan Edwards*, vol. 19, *Sermons and Discourses, 1734–1738*, ed. M. X. Lesser (New Haven, CT: Yale University Press, 2001), 780.

Filled with the Fullness

And as this love of Christ becomes real to us—not just something we assent to on paper, but vivid to us—we are, according to the Bible, "filled with all the fullness of God" (Eph. 3:19). With the possible exception of Colossians 2:9–10—"in him the whole fullness of deity dwells bodily, and you have been filled in him"—this is, to me, the most astonishing claim in the Bible.

Who are we—weak, faltering, mixed-motives we—to be filled up with the very fullness of God himself? How can the clay be filled with the fullness of the potter, the plant with the fullness of the gardener, the house with the architect? What breathtaking condescension, what astounding dignifying of us.

Yet this is not something God relents to do, wishing he could be doing something else. Filling up his fallen people with his own fullness is what he delights to do. It is at the center, not the periphery, of what gets him out of bed in the morning, so to speak.

And how does he do this? What is the means by which he fills us with his own fullness? The text tells us: "to know the love of Christ that surpasses knowledge, that you may be filled with all the fullness of God." Knowing Christ's love is the means, and being filled with divine fullness is the purpose.

We are infused with divine plenitude, fullness, buoyancy, joy, as we experience the love of Christ. We don't go out and attain divine fullness. We receive it. This is the surprise of the Christian life. We get traction in our spiritual lives not centrally as we get down to work but as we open up our hands. The Christian life is indeed one of toil and labor. Anyone who tries to tell you otherwise is a false teacher. But we cannot receive what God has to give when our fists are clenched and our eyes shut, concentrating on our own moral exertion. We need to open up our fists and our eyes and lift both heavenward to receive his love.

His Settled Heart, Our Settled Hearts

And so what I want to say in this chapter is that your growth in Christ will go no further than your settledness, way down deep in your heart, that God loves you. That he has pulled you in to his own deepest heart. His affection for his own never wanes, never sours, never cools. Half-hearted is not who he is. That thing about you that makes you wince most only strengthens his delight in embracing you. At your point of deepest shame and regret, that's where Christ loves you the most. The old Puritan Thomas Goodwin wrote that "Christ is love covered over with flesh."[4] It's who he is.

Divine love is not calculating and cautious, like ours. The God of the Bible is unrestrained. If we are united to Jesus Christ, our sins do not cause his love to take a hit. Though our sins will make *us* more miserable, they cause his love to surge forward all the more. Every heart-stabbing poem, every story of rescue, every novel that evokes longings, every reading of Tolkien and Wendell Berry and John Donne and a thousand others who make the tears flow—all are an echo of the love behind all of human history. This love is the power that burst the created order into existence, and most supremely you, the pinnacle of creation. He created you in order to love you. He knit you together with his hands so that he could pull you into his heart.

One day we will stand before him, quietly, unhurriedly, overwhelmed with relief and standing under the felt flood of divine affection in a way we never can here in this life. But in the meantime

4 Thomas Goodwin, *The Heart of Christ* (Edinburgh: Banner of Truth, 2011), 61.

our lifeline to sustain us in this fallen world is that very love and our heart knowledge of it. Knowing this love is what draws us toward God in this life. We can revere his greatness, but it does not draw us to him; his goodness, his love, draws us in.

In other words, we will delight in God no further than we taste his love. Perhaps the greatest theologian to ever write in the English language was the Puritan John Owen. Here's what Owen says about the connection between our growth in grace and the love of God:

> So much as we see of the love of God, so much shall we delight in him, and no more. Every other discovery of God, without this, will but make the soul fly from him; but if the heart be once much taken up with this the eminency of the Father's love, it cannot choose but be overpowered, conquered, and endeared unto him. . . . If the love of a father will not make a child delight in him, what will?[5]

When I tell my five young kids I love them, they shrug and say, "I know, Dad." But they don't. They believe it, but they hardly know it. I cannot hug them tight enough. I can't say it loudly enough. I can't express it often enough. I have blessed frustration at being unable to communicate to them how precious they are to me.

If that is true on a human level, from a sinful father, what must God's love be like at a divine level, from a blazingly holy Father?

We tend to think we're in danger of overstating God's love for us as we receive it as his children. We hold back, not wanting to be too bold, careful to be sure we don't overdo it. But what if my kids acted like that toward me, holding my love at arm's length? It would break my heart.

---

5 John Owen, *Communion with the Triune God*, ed. Kelly M. Kapic and Justin Taylor (Wheaton, IL: Crossway, 2007), 128.

Don't break your Father's heart. Lap it up. Drink it down. Let the holy fire of his love burn hot in your soul. That is his own deep desire.

Experiencing Divine Love

But how? How do we actually experience God's love? How do we open the vents of our hearts to let in the love of God?

There's no great secret here. Christians have been saying the same thing for two thousand years. We experience the love of God as we look at Jesus and God pours the Holy Spirit, who is himself divine love, into our felt experience. I say that the Holy Spirit is himself divine love because Titus 3:5–6 says that God pours out the Spirit onto us, whereas Romans 5:5 says that God pours out (same Greek word) his love onto us. The two texts describe the same experience.

When I say "experience the love of God," I'm not talking about emotions merely, though our emotions are certainly involved. I'm talking about what the old-timers called our affections. By that they meant the felt inner enjoyment of the heart, the soul throb that only God gives, the joyous calm that blankets those who look upon him.

And as we see more clearly the second person of the Trinity—who he is and what he has done—the third person of the Trinity creates in us an experience of divine love. Just as the sun gives both light and warmth, you could think of the Son as giving light and the Spirit as giving heat. And it is this experience that uglifies sin in our eyes and beautifies righteousness. It is this experience that takes us deeper into communion with God. It is this experience that uproots sin.

We see this in a text such as 1 Corinthians 2:12: "We have received not the spirit of the world, but the Spirit who is from God, that we might understand the things freely given us by God." The English words "things freely given" translate one Greek word, and it's the verb form of the noun for "grace." The Spirit's job is to open our eyes to that with which we have been graced—namely, the atoning work of (as the passage has just identified him) "the Lord of glory" (1 Cor. 2:8), Jesus Christ. Or as Jesus himself says in John 15, the Spirit "will bear witness about me" (v. 26). We'll return to this work of the Spirit in chapter 9, but I must briefly mention it here as we discuss experiencing divine love since the Spirit is the agent by whom this happens.

Look at Christ and see, in him, the love of God displayed. As Owen says, "Exercise your thoughts upon this very thing, the eternal, free, and fruitful love of the Father, and see if your hearts be not wrought upon to delight in him."[6] But where do we look to see Jesus so that the Holy Spirit can be poured afresh into our actual experience? We open a Bible. We see Jesus walking across the pages of the Gospels, but more than that we see him walking across the pages of all the Bible, Genesis to Revelation. For the whole Bible is a united storyline of our need for a Savior and of God's provision of one. So open up your Bible, and get good books to aid you in understanding it. Ask God to reveal himself ever more deeply to you. Ask the Father to take you into clarity about the Son and thus to be warmed by the Spirit.

The famous evangelist from Chicago D. L. Moody was discouraged in his ministry during a visit to New York City. While there he had such an experience of the love of God that, he recounted, he had to ask God to stay his hand. Well, you say, that's a great Christian. That's Moody! The man who led thousands to Christ. What about me? Messy, faltering me? I'm so unlovely.

The answer to that kind of thinking is that your awareness of your unloveliness is precisely why you qualify to experience Ephesians 3

6 Owen, *Communion with the Triune God*, 128.

and the endless love of Christ. If you saw yourself as lovely, that would limit how loved you could feel. But love by its very nature is not dependent on the loveliness of the beloved. If you felt yourself to be lovely, you could feel loved to a degree, but you could not be astonished with how loved you are. It's precisely our messiness that makes Christ's love so surprising, so startling, so arresting—and thereby so transforming.

The surprising nature of God's love is what Jonathan Edwards was reflecting on when he preached:

> They that find Christ [discover that] though he be so glorious and excellent a person, yet they find him ready to receive such poor, worthless, hateful creatures as they are, which was unexpected to them. They are surprised with it.
>
> They did not imagine that Christ was such a kind of person, a person of such grace. They heard he was a holy Savior and hated sin, and they did not imagine he would be so ready to receive such vile, wicked creatures as they. They thought he surely would never be willing to accept such provoking sinners, such guilty wretches, those that had such abominable hearts.
>
> But behold, he is not a whit the more backward to receive them for that. They unexpectedly find him with open arms to embrace them, ready forever to forget all their sins as though they had never been. They find that he as it were runs to meet them, and makes them most welcome, and admits them not only to be his servants but his friends. He lifts them out of the dust and sets them on his throne; he makes them the children of God; he speaks peace to them; he cheers and refreshes their hearts; he admits them unto strict union with himself, and gives the most joyful entertainment, and binds himself to them to be their friend forever.

So are they surprised with their entertainment. They never imagined to find Christ a person of such kind of love and grace as this. 'Tis beyond all imagination or conception.[7]

Look at Jesus. Allow yourself to be surprised at how freely and permanently he embraces you. And enjoy the soul serenity that comes as the Holy Spirit fills you afresh.

Blockages to Knowing His Love

And yet it often isn't that simple, is it? Some of us, no matter how much we try, no matter how much Bible we read, find the experience of God's love elusive.

Some of us look at the evidence of our lives, mindful of the pain we've endured, and we do not know how to respond except with cold cynicism. *The love of Christ?* we wonder. *Is this a joke? You're living in la-la land, Dane. This all sounds nice in theory. But look at the wreckage of my life. I know deep down in my bones I was created to be a palace, magnificent and stately. But I'm a pile of bombed-out rubble given the way others have treated me, wronged me, victimized me. My life disproves the love of Christ.*

If you are having thoughts like that as you hear of Christ's love, I want you to know that you're looking at the wrong life. *Your* life doesn't *disprove* Christ's love; *his* life *proves* it.

In heaven, the eternal Son of God was "palatial" magnificence if anything ever was. But he became a man and, instead of ruling in glorious authority as one would expect of God-become-man, he was rejected and killed. His own life was reduced to bombed-out rubble.

---

7 Jonathan Edwards, "Seeking After Christ," in *The Works of Jonathan Edwards*, vol. 22, *Sermons and Discourses, 1739–1742*, ed. Harry S. Stout and Nathan O. Hatch, with Kyle P. Farley (New Haven, CT: Yale University Press, 2003), 290; language slightly updated.

Why? So that he could sweep sinful you into his deepest heart and never let you go, having satisfied the Father's righteous wrath toward you in his atoning death.

Your suffering does not define you. His does. You have endured pain involuntarily. He has endured pain voluntarily, for you. Your pain is meant to push you to flee to him where he endured what you deserve.

If Jesus himself was willing to journey down into the suffering of hell, you can bank everything on his love as you journey through your own suffering on your way up to heaven.

For others of you, it isn't so much what you have received at the hands of others but your own sin and folly that cause you to doubt God's love. You are a follower of Jesus and you keep messing up. You wonder when the reservoir of divine love is going to run dry.

Here's what I say to you: Do you realize how God treats his children who mistreat his love?

He loves them all the fiercer.

It's who he is. He is love. He is a fountain of affection. He is tireless, unquitting, in his embrace. In a 1948 letter to his congregation the Scottish pastor William Still wrote: "God never tires of giving. Even when we are not grateful, He gives and gives, and gives again. Sometimes when others have grieved Him, as we think, we suppose that God will visit them, punish them or deal hardly with them. Instead He lavishes more tokens of His love upon them."[8]

Let him love you all over again. Pick yourself up off the ground, stop feeling sorry for yourself, and allow his heart to plunge you into his oceanic love more deeply than he ever has before.

---

8   William Still, *Letters of William Still: With an Introductory Biographical Sketch*, ed. Sinclair B. Ferguson (Edinburgh: Banner of Truth, 1984), 35.

Whether the wreckage of your life is your own doing or someone else's, you who are in Christ have never stepped outside the cascading waterfall of divine love. God would have to un-God himself for that deluge to run dry. You have muted your experience of his love. But you cannot stop the flow any more than a single pebble can slow Victoria Falls, a mile across and 360 feet high, as those millions of gallons of the Zambezi River come crashing over the cliffs there in southern Zambia.

Whether you have ignored it, neglected it, squandered it, misunderstood it, or hardened yourself to it—the Lord Jesus Christ approaches you today not with arms crossed but with arms open, the very position in which he hung on the cross, and he says to you:

None of that matters right now. Don't give it another thought.

All that matters now is you and me.

You know you are a mess. You are a sinner. Your entire existence has been built around you.

Step in out of that storm. Let your heart crack open to Joy.

I was punished so that you don't have to be. I was arrested so you could go free. I was indicted so you could be exonerated. I was executed so you could be acquitted.

And all of that is just the beginning of my love. That proved my love, but it's not an endpoint; it's only the doorway into my love.

Humble yourself enough to receive it.

Plunge your parched soul into the sea of my love. There you will find the rest and relief and embrace and friendship your heart longs for.

The wraparound category of your life is not your performance but God's love. The defining hallmark of your life is not your cleanness but his embrace. The deepest destiny of your life is to descend ever deeper, with quiet yet ever-increasing intensity, into the endless love of God. We grow spiritually by getting a head start on that project, right here in this fallen earthly life.

5

Acquittal

WE GROW IN CHRIST AS WE GO DEEPER INTO, rather than moving on from, the verdict of acquittal that got us into Christ in the first place.

It is common in some quarters of the church to think that the message of the gospel initiates us into the Christian life, and then we move on to other strategies when it comes to growing in Christ. This is a fundamental mistake. We will never grow truly as long as we retain this error. My goal in this chapter is to explain how the gospel is not a hotel to pass through but a home to live in. Not only a gateway into the Christian life but the pathway of the Christian life. Not jumper cables to get the Christian life started but an engine to keep the Christian life going.

We could think of it this way: This is a book about sanctification. How do we move forward spiritually? And in this book on sanctification, this chapter is on justification. Sanctification is lifelong, gradual growth in grace. Justification, however, is not a process but an event, a moment in time, the verdict of legal acquittal once and for all. Why then are we thinking about justification in a book about sanctification? Here's why: *the process of sanctification is, in large part, fed by constant returning, ever more deeply, to the event of justification.*

This may sound odd at first. Aren't we going backward if we seek to grow by remembering our initial justification? Not any more than a train passenger, when asked by the steward to see his ticket again, pulls out the ticket that initially got him onto the train. That ticket got him on but is also what is needed to keep him on the train.

But let's be more specific, bearing in mind that growth in Christ is a matter of transformation from the inside out, as opposed to merely externally oriented behavioral conformity. We could put the point of this chapter in three sentences:

1. Justification is outside-in, and we lose it if we make it inside-out.
2. Sanctification is inside-out, and we lose it if we make it outside-in.
3. And this inside-out sanctification is largely fed by daily appropriation of this outside-in justification.

Justification

First, justification is outside-in, and we lose it if we make it inside-out.

Here's what I mean. Justification is "outside-in" in the sense that we are justified by being given a right standing that comes to us from wholly outside us. This is strange and difficult to get our minds around at first. The very notion of a person's standing, an assessment of whether someone is guilty or innocent, universally depends on his or her own performance. Yet in the gospel we are given what the Reformers called an "alien righteousness" because the record of Jesus is given to us. In what Luther called the "happy exchange," we are given Christ's righteous record and he takes on our sin-ridden record; accordingly, we are treated as innocent and Christ was treated as guilty, bearing our punishment on the cross. We are thus "justified"—that is, declared faultless with respect to our legal standing. Despite being the offending parties, despite having no case to make out on our behalf based on our own merits, we are free to leave the courtroom. And no one can ever accuse us again. And this justifying verdict is something we can receive only by acknowledging that we don't deserve it and asking for Christ's record to stand in for ours.

We resist this through and through. Accepting this state of affairs strikes at our most deeply entrenched intuitions about the way the world works. We resist it not merely because it strikes at our pride, though that is true. More deeply, it seems to throw off our moral compass about who we are and how we can feel stable about our place in the universe. The Bible's teaching on justification by faith feels like moral vertigo, as if up is down and down is up. For we are being told to stop doing what is our inveterate inclination—to look inside to answer the questions Am I okay? Do I matter? What is the verdict over my life? Am I at peace with my Maker?

The great teachers of the past understood how heart-contrary we are to accepting wholesale the surprise of justification. This is why the Scottish pastor Robert Murray McCheyne said, "For every one look at yourself, take ten looks at Christ."[1] It's why John Newton said that a single view of Christ "will do you more good than poring over your own wounds for a month."[2] And they were simply following Scripture's lead: "looking to Jesus," as Hebrews 12:2 puts it. We tend to look within to answer the greatest question of the soul, Am I right with God? We do not ask it that baldly, of course. We take refuge in the truth of justification—*mostly*, anyway—while our hearts

---

1 In Andrew A. Bonar, *Memoirs and Remains of the Rev. Robert Murray McCheyne* (Edinburgh: Oliphant, Anderson, and Ferrier, 1892), 293.
2 *Letters of John Newton* (Edinburgh: Banner of Truth, 2007), 380.

find subtle ways of undermining what our minds confess on paper. We receive the truth of justification but gently strengthen it through our performance, generally without consciously realizing what we're doing.

But to do this—to quietly confirm God's verdict of "not guilty" over us through our own contribution—is to cause the entire doctrine of justification to fall to pieces and to become impotent in our daily lives. To do this is, in biblical terms, to "rebuild" what we "tore down" (Gal. 2:18). We "tore down" our own righteousness and all the futility of trying to establish it out of our own resources. Why "rebuild" it? This would be to "nullify the grace of God" (Gal. 2:21). To do this is to turn justification from an outside-in truth to an inside-out truth. But we lose entirely the comfort of justification if it is vulnerable to any self-strengthening. It must be all or nothing.

Sanctification

Second, sanctification is inside-out, and we lose it if we make it outside-in.

Our growth in godliness, in other words, works in an inverse way to justification, both in how it works and in how it gets ruined. In our justification the verdict of legal acquittal must come wholly from heaven, landing on us as something earned by someone outside us, in no way helped out by our contribution. But that has to do with our *standing*. That is the objective result of the gospel. Sanctification, however, is change with regard to our *walk*, our personal holiness, the subjective result of the gospel. This must happen internally.

And just as we ruin the comfort of justification if we make it internal, we ruin the reality of sanctification if we make it external. Just as we are tempted to strengthen our justified state through internal contribution, so we are tempted to strengthen our sanctification through external rules.

But growth in godliness is not generated by conformity to any external code—whether the Ten Commandments or the commands of Jesus or self-imposed rules or your own conscience. This does not mean the commands of Scripture are worthless. On the contrary, they are "holy and righteous and good" (Rom. 7:12). But the commands of the Bible are the steering wheel, not the engine, to your growth. They are vitally instructive, but they do not themselves give you the power you need to obey the instruction.

Think of how we grow physically. I don't ask my six-year-old daughter, Chloe, to take her lunch and smear it all over her body. I tell her to eat it. The food needs to get inside her, not remain on the outside. One of the great mistakes made generation after generation through church history is to slather rules onto our behavior and think that external behavior is what fosters, or even accurately reflects, vital spiritual growth. This is the mistake of the Pharisees, who "clean the *outside* of the cup and plate, but *inside* they are full of greed and self-indulgence" (Matt. 23:25). They are "like whitewashed tombs, which *outwardly* appear beautiful, but *within* are full of dead people's bones and all uncleanness" (Matt. 23:27).

Or consider one of the most astonishing texts in the New Testament. Before we look at it, let me ask, what do you picture when you hear the word *godliness*? I'm going to guess it doesn't look like the picture Paul paints in 2 Timothy of what people will be like in the time between Christ's first and second comings, where he gives the longest vice list in the New Testament:

People will be lovers of self, lovers of money, proud, arrogant, abusive, disobedient to their parents, ungrateful, unholy, heartless, unappeasable, slanderous, without self-control, brutal, not loving good, treacherous, reckless, swollen with conceit, lovers of pleasure rather than lovers of God. (3:2–4)

That's eighteen vices. The list is suffocating in its rising portrait of wickedness.

But there's a nineteenth trait on the list, one last mark of the spiritual bankruptcy the church must be wary of: "having the appearance of godliness, but denying its power" (3:5).

Having the appearance of godliness. Apparently being a lover of self can look like godliness. Being a lover of money can look like godliness. Someone can be filled with pride and arrogance all the while presented as godliness. One can be ungrateful, unholy, heartless, unappeasable—and to the outside observer it looks like godliness.

True sanctification, true growth in holiness, is internal. It will *manifest* itself on the outside; "The tree is known by its fruit" (Matt. 12:33). But the tree creates the fruit; the fruit does not create the tree. Edward Fisher, in his famous Puritan treatise on sanctification, explained that external conformity to rules without an internal reality fueling it is akin to watering every part of a tree except its roots and expecting it to grow.[3] The internal realities of the Christian are what define true growth in Christ.

Sanctification by Justification

Third, inside-out sanctification is largely fed by daily appropriation of outside-in justification.

---

3   Edward Fisher, *The Marrow of Modern Divinity* (Pittsburgh: Paxton, 1830), 227 (pt. 1, chap. 3, sec. 8: "Evan: 'The truth is, many preachers stand upon the praise of some moral virtue, and do inveigh against some vice of the times, more than upon pressing men to believe. . . . as if a man should water all the tree, and not the root'").

The outside-in verdict nurtures the inside-out process. You can't crowbar your way into change. You can only be melted. Reflection on the wonder of the gospel—that we are justified simply by looking away from self to the finished work of Christ on our behalf—softens our hearts. The labor of sanctification becomes wonderfully calmed. The gospel is what changes us, and only it can, because the gospel itself is telling us what is true of us before we ever begin to change, and no matter how slowly our change comes. (In saying this I do not mean to collapse all that the gospel says into the one category of justification; the gospel is broader than justification, including other glorious doctrines such as adoption, reconciliation, redemption, and so on. But justification is the sharpest edge of the gospel because it is the doctrine where the sheer gratuity of the grace of the gospel stands forth most clearly.)

We intuitively think that the way to grow is to hear exhortation. That is normal and natural to the human mind. And exhortation has an important place. We need it. We are not mature Christians if we can never bear to hear the challenges and commands of Scripture. But the Bible teaches that healthy spiritual growth takes place only when such commands land on those who know they are accepted and safe irrespective of the degree to which they successfully keep those commands. Or to put it differently, in line with the broader point of this whole book: we grow by going *deeper* into the justification that forgave us in the first place.

Here's how the church historian and theologian of revival Richard Lovelace puts it in his classic work on spiritual renewal:

> Much that we have interpreted as a defect of sanctification in church people is really an outgrowth of their loss of bearing with respect to justification. Christians who are no longer sure that God

loves and accepts them in Jesus, apart from their present spiritual achievements, are subconsciously radically insecure persons—much less secure than non-Christians, because they have too much light to rest easily under the constant bulletins they receive from their Christian environment about the holiness of God and the righteousness they are supposed to have.[4]

This need to return constantly to the freeness of the doctrine of justification must be emphasized because the fall rewires us to do precisely the opposite. Our fallen hearts are spring-loaded to assess our justified state on the basis of how our sanctification is going. But we grow in Christ by placing our sanctification in the light of our justification. The old English pastor Thomas Adam, who served a single church for fifty-eight years, reflected on this truth in his diary, which was published in 1814 after his death, and he called it "sanctification by justification." He wrote: "Justification by sanctification is man's way to heaven. . . . Sanctification by justification is God's."[5]

Indeed, many thinkers down through the corridors of church history could be brought forth here who have taught that we will move forward in the Christian life by *not* moving past the truth that forgave us in the first place. Martin Luther defined progressive sanctification as "the doctrine of the godliness which is caused by the justification of the heart."[6] Francis Turretin taught that "justification itself (which brings the remission of sins) does not carry with it the permission or license to sin (as the Epicureans hold), but ought to enkindle the desire of piety

4 Richard Lovelace, *Dynamics of Spiritual Life: An Evangelical Theology of Renewal* (Downers Grove, IL: InterVarsity Press, 1979), 211–12.

5 Thomas Adam, *Private Thoughts on Religion* (Glasgow: Collins, 1824), 199.

6 In Ewald M. Plass, *What Luther Says: A Practical in-Home Anthology for the Active Christian* (St. Louis: Concordia, 1959), 720.

and the practice of holiness. . . . Thus justification stands related to sanctification as the means to the end."[7] Thomas Chalmers famously preached, "The freer the gospel, the more sanctifying the gospel; and the more it is received as a doctrine of grace, the more will it be felt as a doctrine according to godliness."[8] In his classic work on union with Christ, James Stewart wrote: "It is God's justifying verdict itself which sanctifies. . . . It is precisely because God waits for no guarantees but pardons out-and-out . . . that forgiveness regenerates, and justification sanctifies."[9] Reformed stalwart Herman Bavinck defined real faith as

> a practical knowledge of the grace that God has revealed in Christ, a heartfelt trust that he has forgiven all our sins and accepted us as his children. For that reason this faith is not only needed at the beginning in justification, but it must also accompany the Christian throughout one's entire life, and also play a permanent and irreplaceable role in sanctification.[10]

Dutch theologian G. C. Berkouwer argues repeatedly throughout his study of sanctification that "the heart of sanctification is the life which feeds on . . . justification."[11]

We could equally go to the great Reformed confessions to find a similar note struck. The Belgic Confession asserts that "far from

---

7   Francis Turretin, *Institutes of Elenctic Theology*, ed. James T. Dennison, trans. George Musgrave Giger, 3 vols. (Phillipsburg, NJ: P&R, 1992–1997), 2:692–93.

8   Thomas Chalmers, "The Expulsive Power of a New Affection," in *Sermons and Discourses*, 2 vols. (New York: Robert Carter, 1844), 2:277.

9   James S. Stewart, *A Man in Christ: The Vital Elements of St. Paul's Religion* (New York: Harper & Row, 1935), 258–60.

10 Herman Bavinck, *Reformed Dogmatics*, vol. 2, *God and Creation*, ed. John Bolt, trans. John Vriend (Grand Rapids, MI: Baker, 2004), 257.

11 G. C. Berkouwer, *Faith and Sanctification*, trans. John Vriend, Studies in Dogmatics (Grand Rapids, MI: Eerdmans, 1952), 93.

making people cold toward living in a pious and holy way, this justifying faith, quite to the contrary, so works within them that apart from it they will never do a thing out of love for God but only out of love for themselves and fear of being condemned" (article 24). The Canons of Dort speak of the way in which God preserves his people: "Just as it has pleased God to begin this work of grace in us by the proclamation of the gospel, so he preserves, continues, and completes his work by the hearing and reading of the gospel, by meditation on it" (5.14).

Yet the final arbiter in all this is not any historical figure or creed but Scripture. The most striking example of how the freeness of our salvation itself transforms us is in Galatians 2.

Justification and Fear

What is the internal logic by which a verdict of acquittal changes us from the inside out? The text reads:

> When Cephas came to Antioch, I opposed him to his face, because he stood condemned. For before certain men came from James, he was eating with the Gentiles; but when they came he drew back and separated himself, fearing the circumcision party. And the rest of the Jews acted hypocritically along with him, so that even Barnabas was led astray by their hypocrisy. But when I saw that their conduct was not in step with the truth of the gospel, I said to Cephas before them all, "If you, though a Jew, live like a Gentile and not like a Jew, how can you force the Gentiles to live like Jews?"
>
> We ourselves are Jews by birth and not Gentile sinners; yet we know that a person is not justified by works of the law but through faith in Jesus Christ, so we also have believed in Christ Jesus, in

order to be justified by faith in Christ and not by works of the law, because by works of the law no one will be justified. (Gal. 2:11–16)

A lot could be mined from this fascinating interchange between Paul and Peter. I want to make just one observation. Why would Paul address an internal church conflict with the doctrine of justification?

We tend to think of justification by faith as a key truth to get us *into* the Christian life. Why did Paul reach into his theological toolkit and pull out this doctrine to fix a problem among those who were already believers? Here we have Paul, a believer, writing to the Galatians, who were believers, about an episode involving Peter, a believer, because of his withdrawing from Gentile believers when Jewish-raised believers from James arrived. And it is here in this internal church conflict, not in an evangelistic speech in Acts, that we have the Bible's most famous verse on justification by faith (Gal. 2:16).

Why justification? Why didn't Paul speak of sanctification? Or the Holy Spirit? Or the need for love?

Why did Paul say that Peter and Barnabas withdrawing from the Gentile Christians was conduct "not in step with the truth of the gospel" (v. 14)? Why did Paul not say that they were "not walking by the Spirit" or that their "conduct was not in step with the growth they should be cultivating"? And this was no isolated biblical instance. All over the New Testament the apostles brought the gospel to bear on believers' lives. Paul told the Roman Christians, "I am eager to preach the gospel to you" (Rom. 1:15); he exhorted the Colossian believers to live "not shifting from the hope of the gospel" (Col. 1:23); and he reminded the Corinthian believers that they were to "stand" in and "hold fast to" the gospel (1 Cor. 15:1–2). Apparently the apostles considered the gospel not a one-time vaccination that spares us from hell but food to nourish us all the way to heaven.

The key to understanding what was happening among the Galatians is tucked in at the very end of Galatians 2:12: "fearing the circumcision party." The dynamic at work when the believers from James showed up from Jerusalem and Peter and Barnabas stopped having lunch with the non-Jewish believers—the reality simmering beneath the surface of Peter's actions—was fear.

Fear of what? Not persecution. Remember, everyone present was a follower of Christ. Given the sweep of the whole book of Galatians, Peter must have been afraid of losing the same thing that Paul said he wasn't afraid of losing back in chapter 1: "Am I now seeking the approval of man, or of God? Or am I trying to please man? If I were still trying to please man, I would not be a servant of Christ" (1:10). Peter feared losing the approval of people.

That was a defect with regard to his ongoing growth in grace. Peter had been a follower of Christ for many years. His was a sanctification problem. And yet Paul brought justification to bear on it. He lanced Peter's wound with the surgical doctrine of justification by faith. Paul went to the root.

Paul identified Peter's conduct as being out of step with the gospel (2:14) and in violation of the doctrine of justification by faith (2:16) because *Peter had allowed the approval of people to erode his grasp of the approval that the gospel gives and the settled status that justification provides.*

At conversion we understand the gospel for the first time, and we feel the immense relief of being forgiven of our sins and granted a new status in the family of God. We learn for the first time that we are legally acquitted, innocent, free to leave the courtroom. But even for Christians, there remain regions within that continue to resist the grace of the gospel without our even realizing it. And one vital aspect of growing in Christ is coming back time and again to the doctrine of justification to do chemotherapy on the remaining malignancies of our craving for human approval. To put it differently, at conversion we walk *out* of the courtroom, but throughout our lives of discipleship we suffer from gospel amnesia and keep walking *back in*.

In August of 2013 a Nigerian newspaper released a story containing an account of precisely what we all tend to do:

> An inmate caused a mild farce at the Owerri High Court after a judge acquitted him of all charges against him, but he refused and demanded to go back to prison. Instead of the usual jubilation that follow[s] any ruling of "discharged and acquitted," the inmate in question headed straight back to the Prison, only to be intercepted by a prison guard who reminded him he was free to go home. To the chagrin of eyewitnesses, he said he was going nowhere, demanding to be allowed re-entry into the prison.
>
> What seemed like a mild drama turned absurd when the calm of the court premises was shattered by the freed prisoner's shouts and pleas to be allowed to go back to prison, as he thrashed about and struggled with several prison officials. According to eyewitnesses, it took the effort of over six prison officials, court workers, and policemen to get the freed inmate out of the court premises.[12]

That's a picture of us all. We are freed, but we find subtle ways of returning to the prison of self-established standing before God in the divine courtroom. Healthy Christians discipline themselves to never cease hitting "refresh" on the URL of their settled status, the verdict of final acquittal. We have been "approved by God" (1 Thess. 2:4).

Do we realize why our moods are so often dictated by how people respond to us? Why do we get so fretful about our grades in school or

---

12 See "Home Is Where the Heart Is: Freed Inmate Refused to Leave Prison," 360nobs, July 19, 2013, http://360nobs.blogspot.com/2013/07/home-is-where-heart-is-freed-inmate.html.

our job reviews at work or what our parents will think of our home or kids? Why is there that pervasive, slow-burn anxiety boiling within whenever we are at social gatherings? There may be psychological or even physiological factors at play for some of us, I understand, so we should not be simplistic here. But generally the root issue is that we have allowed ourselves imperceptibly to slide away from a heart grasp of the doctrine of justification. Fear has risen in our mental horizon as Galatians 2:16 has faded. We need to realize that the gospel is not only the door into the Christian life but also the living room of the Christian life. Justification is not a spark plug that ignites the Christian life but an engine that powers it all along the way. Few of us would testify that we have been tempted to eat according to kosher Jewish dietary regulations, but all of us who know our own hearts know exactly what Peter was feeling in his desire to retain the approval of others and in his fear of losing it.

What we all tend to do is walk through life amassing a sense of who we are as an aggregate of what we think everyone else thinks of us. We walk along, building a sense of self through all the feedback pinging back at us. We don't even realize we're doing it. And when others are critical, or snub us, or ignore us, or ridicule us, that builds our sense of who we are. It inevitably shapes us. And so we must constantly hold the gospel before our eyes. And as the gospel becomes *real* to us, the need for human approval loses its vice-like grip on our hearts, because we're no longer putting our heads down on our pillows at night medicating our sense of worth with human approval. The doctrine of justification frees us not only from the judgment of God in the future but also from the judgment of people in the present.

So what I am trying to say in this chapter on "acquittal" is that if we long to grow in Christ, we dare not do what comes so naturally— namely, *say* we believe that the verdict over our lives is decisively settled in our justified status before God but then move on to other ideas and strategies when it comes to our emotional lives and daily pressures. For if we do, we will find our lives riddled with fear. We will be paralyzed with anxieties, because we will be afraid that our functional god will condemn us—not justify us—if we fail it. We are fearful of not succeeding in a job, or not impressing someone we respect, or botching the date, or failing the test, or missing the shot. We fantasize about succeeding in those real-life situations and have nightmares about failing. Why? Because we treat the gospel as the ignition but not the sustaining reality to our inner life. We are not walking "in step with the truth of the gospel." We haven't let the radioactive nature of the doctrine of justification by faith destroy our malignant need for human approval. Sensing our inadequacy, we set up our career, our relationships, our studies, our public speaking, our athletic abilities as functional gods to which we are looking for justification—*to know we're okay.*

But what if we went into the interview, the conversation, the classroom, the game, already okay? Already justified. Not just theologically but emotionally. Not just in our mind but in our gut. We would be world shakers. The old Presbyterian theologian J. Gresham Machen put it movingly in 1925.

> I am not at all ashamed to speak, even in this day and generation, of "the doctrine of justification by faith." It should not be supposed, however, that that doctrine is an abstruse thing. On the contrary it is . . . instinct with life. It is an answer to the greatest personal question ever asked by a human soul—the question: "How shall I be right with God; how do I stand in God's sight; with what favor does he look upon me?"

There are those, it must be admitted, who never raise that question; there are those who are concerned with the question of their standing before men, but never with the question of their standing before God; there are those who are interested in what "people say," but not in the question what God says. Such men, however, are not those who move the world; they are apt to go with the current; they are apt to do as others do; they are not the heroes who change the destinies of the race.[13]

Justification and Idolatry

What we have really been talking about is idolatry, which is the flip side to justification by faith. Human approval is one common idol, but we look to many pseudo gods for that final verdict to know we are okay and we matter, to get that elusive sigh of the soul. Diagnostic questions to expose our idols are questions such as

- What does my mind tend to drift back to when I lie awake in bed?
- What do I spend disposable income on?
- What in other people do I tend to envy?
- What is that one thing that, if God were to appear to me today and tell me I would never have it, would make life feel not worth living?
- If I'm married, what would my spouse say I tend to give myself to that makes him or her feel neglected?
- How would my heart—not my theology, but my heart—phrase the hymn, "When _____, it is well with my soul"?
- What do I find myself praying for that is nowhere promised in the Bible?

13 J. Gresham Machen, *What Is Faith?* (repr., Grand Rapids, MI: Eerdmans, 1979), 163.

By no means do the answers to these questions necessarily reveal idols in our hearts. But they're intended to help draw to the surface what may be competing for our hearts' deepest loyalty, quietly displacing Christ and the comprehensive comfort of the gospel. Idolatry is the folly of asking a gift to be a giver.

And here's the point I want to make: *These are justification questions.* Idolatry is simply pseudo justification. It is asking a created thing rather than the Creator to render a verdict over me. We think, *As long as I get that, then I'll have arrived; then I can handle anything.* The problem is that unlike the gospel, idols nurture an insatiable itch. The more we scratch, the more the itch spreads. Pursuing the idol causes the idol to keep moving just further out of reach. In that rare instance where we do in fact attain the idol we've longed for, we will be astonished at how empty and hollow it is. All of this world's fraudulent pseudo justifications are shiny on the outside but only bring misery when attained. They are like baited fish hooks: when bit down on, they only bring pain.

Anyone remotely in touch with reality walks this earth acutely aware of the deep inadequacy within, the sense of not measuring up. And we medicate that deep, nagging sense of insufficiency through the swelling bank account, the perfect face, the sculpted body, the number of social media followers, the reputation, the beautiful spouse, the famous friends, the sense of humor, the appearance of intelligence, the political outmaneuvering and one-upmanship, the sexual exploits, or even the upstanding moral resume. We feel our nakedness and seek to be "clothed" by these accomplishments. We seek to be *justified* by these things. And as surely as the Galatians claimed Christ as their Savior but slipped in circumcision as a justification enhancement and thereby emptied the gospel of its power, so we claim Christ as our Savior but slip in our own favorite idol and thereby empty the gospel of its power.

Every idol is man-made. Every false justification is generated by us. But God himself has come to us with a justification of his own doing. It is the atoning verdict of Jesus Christ. We can only receive it. To add to it is therefore to subtract from it. We simply breathe it in with a heart posture of trusting faith. And thereby God justifies us—God himself. Our okay-ness, our record, our identity, our significance, are no longer in our hands, not even a little.

It was Martin Luther who opened my eyes to this. More than once throughout his writings he points out that the first of the Ten Commandments is the prohibition of idolatry: "You shall have no other gods before me" (Ex. 20:3). Luther explains that the first commandment is in essence a call to justification by faith; that is, justification by God. Negatively, we are to avoid idolatry. Positively, we are to trust in God. An idol, after all, is not simply a matter of what we worship but, more deeply, what we *trust* (Ps. 115:4–8). Consequently, there is no breaking of commandments 2–10 without at the same time breaking commandment 1. To commit adultery is to break commandments 1 and 7, because it is to make sex an idol in which we trust to fulfill and complete us. We are not leaving our existence, our justification, in God's hands. To steal is to violate commandments 1 and 8, because we are not resting in God's provision of finances. We are not exercising faith in him alone. And so on.[14]

14 Martin Luther, "A Treatise on Good Works," in *The Christian in Society I*, in *Luther's Works*, ed. Jaroslav Pelikan and Helmut T. Lehmann, 55 vols. (Philadelphia: Fortress, 1955–1986), 44:30–34.

Live your life out of the fullness of a justified existence. Honor the first commandment. Do not be an idolater. Let Jesus Christ clothe you, dignify you, justify you. Nothing else can.

Three Closing Portraits

Everything I've said in this chapter has been fairly theoretical. So I'd like to close by showing how the truth we've been exploring here was experienced in a deeply personal way by three figures in history: Martin Luther (1483–1546), C. S. Lewis (1898–1963), and Francis Schaeffer (1912–1984).

I've already mentioned Luther a few times in this chapter, and you can pretty much parachute anywhere into his writings, start reading, and before long find him extolling the comforts of the gospel—especially justification—as vital ingredients for the Christian's life and growth. Luther had spent some of his early years as a monk, praying and doing menial work and pursuing simplicity, yearning to scrub his conscience clean as he scrubbed the floors of the monastery clean. He couldn't. No one can. The conscience is unappeasable short of the verdict of full acquittal on the basis of Christ's finished work, received through the hungry, empty hands of faith, apart from any human contribution.

And it was in Luther's study of the New Testament that the gospel broke open to him. Luther understood the powerful natural reflex of the human heart toward works righteousness. He came to see with particular insight that all people are spring-loaded to seek to strengthen God's favor through their performance, and that therefore it is not only our badness that needs repenting of but also our goodness. He saw this subtle but profound insistence on contributing to our standing before God as something at odds with his Bible though engrained in himself and endorsed by the Roman Catholic Church.

Preaching on John 14:6, for example ("I am the way"), Luther said:

Christ is not only the way on which we must begin our journey, but He is also the right and the safe way we must walk to the end. We dare not be deflected from this. . . . Here Christ wants to say: "When you have apprehended Me in faith, you are on the right way, which is reliable. But only see that you remain and continue on it." . . . Christ wants to tear and turn our hearts from all trust in anything else and pin them to Himself alone.[15]

But it was especially in his commentary on Galatians that Luther saw and taught this need to stay fixed on the freeness of the gospel our whole lives long. In a representative comment on Galatians 1:6—"I am astonished that you are so quickly deserting him who called you in the grace of Christ and are turning to a different gospel"—Luther said:

The matter of justification is brittle—not in itself, for it is most sure and certain, but in respect to us, within us. I myself have experienced this, for I sometimes wrestle in hours of darkness. I know how often I suddenly lose the beams of the Gospel and grace. It is as though thick dark clouds obscured them from me. So I know about the slippery place in which we stand, even if we are experienced and seem to be surefooted in matters of faith. . . . So, let every faithful person work hard to learn and retain this doctrine: and to that end, let us pray humbly and heartily, and study and meditate continually on the Word.[16]

---

15 Martin Luther, *Sermons on the Gospel of St. John 14–16*, in *Luther's Works*, 24:47–48, 50.

16 In Alister McGrath and J. I. Packer, eds., *Galatians by Martin Luther*, Crossway Classic Commentaries (Wheaton, IL: Crossway, 1998), 57–58.

Far less known is the late-in-life awakening to the gospel that C. S. Lewis experienced. Many of us know of his famous conversion, his profound literary accomplishments, his extensive correspondence and meetings with his fellow Inklings, his High Church Anglicanism, and his all-too-brief marriage. But are we aware that the reality of the forgiveness of the gospel came home to him in a decisive and permanently transforming way?

It happened on April 25, 1951. Later that year Lewis wrote a letter to an Italian priest who had struck up a correspondence with him. The priest had read an Italian translation of Lewis's book *The Screwtape Letters* and, not knowing English, wrote Lewis a letter of appreciation in Latin. Lewis, proficient in Latin, received the letter and wrote back in Latin. The two enjoyed a back-and-forth for several years in this way. In December 1951 Lewis wrote to this priest:

> During the past year a great joy has befallen me. Difficult though it is, I shall try to explain this in words. It is astonishing that sometimes we believe that we believe what, really, in our heart, we do not believe.
>
> For a long time I believed that I believed in the forgiveness of sins. But suddenly (on St. Mark's Day) this truth appeared in my mind in so clear a light that I perceived that never before (and that after many confessions and absolutions) had I believed it with my whole heart.
>
> So great is the difference between mere affirmation by the intellect and that faith, fixed in the very marrow and as it were palpable, which the Apostle wrote was *substance*.
>
> Perhaps I was granted this deliverance in response to your intercessions on my behalf!

This emboldens me to say to you something that a layman ought scarcely to say to a priest nor a junior to a senior. (On the other hand, *out of the mouths of babes*: indeed, as once to Balaam, out of the mouth of an ass!) It is this you write too much about your own sins. Beware (permit me, my dearest Father, to say beware) lest humility should pass over into anxiety or sadness. It is bidden us to 'rejoice and always rejoice'. Jesus has cancelled the handwriting that was against us. Lift up our hearts![17]

This is a striking report to read from Lewis, not least because he was fifty-three years old. One might wonder if it was a temporary season of renewed appreciation of the gospel, nothing more. But a close reading of the entire volume of his letters during these years reveals that this was a defining moment in his life, because he comes back to this experience throughout his letters, even several years after the experience.

In 1954, for example, he writes to a certain "Mrs. Jessup" of his 1951 experience as a revolutionary change "from mere intellectual acceptance of, to realisation of, the doctrine that our sins are forgiven. That is perhaps the most blessed thing that has ever happened to me. How little they know of Christianity who think that the story *ends* with conversion."[18]

In 1956, writing to Mary Van Deusen, he reflects on the gospel by saying: "I had *assented* to the doctrine years earlier and would have said I believed it. Then, one blessed day, it suddenly became real to me and made what I had previously called 'belief' look absolutely unreal."[19]

17 C. S. Lewis, *The Collected Letters of C. S. Lewis*, vol. 3, *Narnia, Cambridge, and Joy, 1950–1963*, ed. Walter Hooper (San Francisco: HarperOne, 2007), 151–52.
18 Lewis, *Collected Letters*, 3:425.
19 Lewis, *Collected Letters*, 3:751; emphasis original.

Writing to Mary Shelburne in 1958 he says, "I had been a Christian for many years before I *really* believed in the forgiveness of sins, or more strictly, before my theoretical belief became a reality to me."[20] He writes her again the next year and responds to a comment she made about the difficulty of feeling that we are not worthy to be forgiven by saying to her:

> You surely don't mean 'feeling that we are not *worthy* to be forgiven'? For of course we aren't. Forgiveness by its nature is for the unworthy. You mean feeling that we *are not* forgiven. I have known that. I 'believed' theoretically in the divine forgiveness for years before it really came home to me. It is a wonderful moment when it does.[21]

All this is startling for a couple reasons. First, Lewis only had twelve years left to live when he had this 1951 experience. He had written most of his books. But it was at this point that the forgiveness of the gospel truly clicked into place for him. Second, Lewis came back to this experience repeatedly over the course of his life. It was not of transient significance. It marked him for life.

Francis Schaeffer experienced a similar post-conversion discovery of the gospel, though in his case it proved to be *the* turning point of his life and ministry. As with Lewis, it happened in 1951, though Schaeffer was a little younger at the time (thirty-nine). He and his wife, Edith, lived in Switzerland. He describes what happened like this:

> I faced a spiritual crisis in my own life. I had become a Christian from agnosticism many years ago. After that I had become a pastor

---

20 Lewis, *Collected Letters*, 3:935; emphasis original.
21 Lewis, *Collected Letters*, 3:1064; emphasis original.

for ten years in the United States, and then for several years my wife, Edith, and I had been working in Europe. During this time I felt a strong burden to stand for the historical Christian position and for the purity of the visible church. Gradually, however, a problem came to me—the problem of reality. This has two parts: first, it seemed to me that among many of those who held the orthodox position one saw little reality in the things that the Bible so clearly says should be the result of Christianity. Second, it gradually grew on me that my reality was less than it had been in the early days after I had become a Christian. I realized that in honesty I had to go back and rethink my whole position.

We were living in Champéry at the time, and I told Edith that for the sake of honesty I had to go all the way back to my agnosticism and think through the whole matter. I'm sure that she prayed much for me in those days. I walked in the mountains when it was clear, and when it was rainy I walked backward and forward in the hayloft of the old chalet in which we lived. I walked, prayed, and thought through what the Scriptures taught, reviewing my own reasons for being a Christian. . . .

I searched through what the Bible said concerning reality as a Christian. Gradually I saw that the problem was that with all the teaching I had received after I was a Christian, I had heard little about what the Bible says about the meaning of the finished work of Christ for our present lives. Gradually the sun came out and the song came. Interestingly enough, although I had written no poetry for many years, in that time of joy and song I found poetry beginning to flow again.[22]

22 Francis A. Schaeffer, *True Spirituality* (Carol Stream, IL: Tyndale, 1971), xxix–xxx.

Schaeffer had gone stale. His joy had dried up, and he was questioning the viability of Christianity at a fundamental level. What got him through? Revisiting the gospel—the simple, wonderful, justifying gospel, which says that we are acquitted of our guilt once and for all on the exclusive basis of the finished work of Christ on the cross. Not only did this help settle his mind philosophically as to the truth of Christianity; it also caused his life to blossom anew. Poetry poured out of him once again. Color and beauty flooded his heart afresh. This experience in his own life, founded on the Bible, became central to his teaching and discipling more broadly. In his foundational book on living the Christian life, *True Spirituality*, he says: "I become a Christian once for all on the basis of the finished work of Christ through faith; that is justification. But the Christian life, sanctification, operates on the same basis, but moment by moment."[23]

For all three men, the reality of the gospel was a personal, transformative truth—not just something about which they theologized. I've deliberately chosen these three figures because they represent three different currents in the Christian river. One is German and the father of Lutheranism, one English and a High Church Anglican, and one an American Presbyterian. More than this, they have made quite different contributions to the church, with distinct emphases and aromas to each one's ministry. Yet each found himself coming back in a post-conversion way to the liberating truth of the same gospel. In this they leave us an example, not simply for our imitation, but so that we can go to the same source that they did—the

23 Schaeffer, *True Spirituality*, 70.

Scriptures and the biblical teaching on divine acquittal through the work of Jesus Christ.

Do you want to grow in Christ? Never graduate beyond the gospel. Move ever deeper into the gospel. The freeness of your outside in justification is a critical ingredient to fostering your inside-out sanctification.

6

Honesty

TO THIS POINT WE HAVE BEEN REFLECTING on what happens between God and me in fostering growth. But to these vertical realities we must join the horizontal. A Christian is connected not only *up*, to God, but also *out*, to other Christians.

An independent Christian is a nonsensical category according to the Bible. Scripture calls believers the body of Christ. That is perhaps a familiar metaphor for many of us, but consider what it must mean. We live our lives in Christ in a way that is vitally, organically joined to all other believers. We who are in Christ are no more detached from other believers than muscle tissue can be detached from ligaments in a healthy body. When you pass another Christian in the grocery store or in the hallway at church, that is a body's hand passing that same body's foot, both of whom are controlled by a single head. They may be different genders, different ethnicities, polar opposite personalities, and seventy years apart in age—but they are far more connected than two siblings from the same family, ethnic background, and DNA, one of whom is in Christ while the other is not. C. S. Lewis put it like this:

> Things which are parts of a single organism may be very different from one another: things which are not, may be very alike. Six

pennies are quite separate and very alike: my nose and my lungs are very different but they are only alive at all because they are parts of my body and share its common life. Christianity thinks of individuals not as mere members of a group or items in a list, but as organs in a body—different from one another and each contributing what no other could.[1]

And one reason the apostles speak of Christians as the body of Christ is to communicate that just as a body grows and matures, Christians are to grow and mature: "we are to grow up in every way into him who is the head, into Christ, from whom the whole body, joined and held together by every joint with which it is equipped, when each part is working properly, makes the body grow so that it builds itself up in love" (Eph. 4:15–16).

The Bible has much to say about how we are to interact with each other as fellow Christians if we are to grow. I'd like to focus in this chapter on one particularly important teaching from the New Testament, the most important corporate reality for our growth in Christ: honesty.

Walking in the Light

If I exhorted you to "walk in the light," what would you instinctively think I'm talking about? Would you think I am exhorting you to live in a morally pure way? That would be a reasonable expectation. But if I spoke of "walking in the light" as the apostle John does, I would be talking about something quite different. Here's what we read in 1 John 1:

---

1 C. S. Lewis, *Mere Christianity* (1952; repr., New York: Touchstone, 1996), 161.

This is the message we have heard from him and proclaim to you, that God is light, and in him is no darkness at all. If we say we have fellowship with him while we walk in darkness, we lie and do not practice the truth. But if we walk in the light, as he is in the light, we have fellowship with one another, and the blood of Jesus his Son cleanses us from all sin. If we say we have no sin, we deceive ourselves, and the truth is not in us. If we confess our sins, he is faithful and just to forgive us our sins and to cleanse us from all unrighteousness. If we say we have not sinned, we make him a liar, and his word is not in us. (1 John 1:5–10)

The key is verse 7: "If we walk in the light, as he is in the light, we have fellowship with one another, and the blood of Jesus his Son cleanses us from all sin."

So, does this text exhort moral purity? The Bible certainly does say this. "Be pure and blameless" (Phil. 1:10). "Keep yourself pure" (1 Tim. 5:22). "Be self-controlled, pure" (Titus 2:5). The apostle John himself clearly desires this for his readers: "My little children, I am writing these things to you that you may not sin" (1 John 2:1). And at first glance it may appear that this is John's point when he speaks of walking in the light in 1:7. After all, he says, "If we walk in the light, *as he is in the light*"—that is, as God is in the light. God is morally pure, so surely we are being called to purity, like him, right?

But the point of this text lies elsewhere. John has something far more liberating to say. Walking in the light in this text is *honesty with other Christians*.

Notice the emphasis of the surrounding verses. "If we *say we have no sin*, we deceive ourselves" (1:8). Then John speaks of confessing our sins—acknowledging honestly our failures: "If we *confess our sins . . .*" (1:9). And then verse 10 returns to the point that verse 8 made: "If we *say we have not* sinned, we make him a liar" (1:10). Apparently walking in the light is confessing our sinfulness, and walking in the darkness is hiding our sinfulness. Walking in the light, in this text, is not primarily avoiding sin but acknowledging it. After all, even verse 7 itself concludes with an assurance of the cleansing blood of Christ—a natural reminder if "walking in the light" earlier in the verse refers to confessing our sins.

Here is what I want to say in this chapter: You are restricting your growth if you do not move through life doing the painful, humiliating, liberating work of cheerfully bringing your failures out from the darkness of secrecy into the light of acknowledgment before a Christian brother or sister. In the darkness, your sins fester and grow in strength. In the light, they wither and die. Walking in the light, in other words, is honesty with God and others.

The classic reflection on walking in the light is Dietrich Bonhoeffer's book *Life Together*. He titles one chapter "Confession and Communion," because his burden is to show the vital link between those two horizontal realities. He opens the chapter by saying:

> He who is alone with his sin is utterly alone. It may be that Christians, notwithstanding corporate worship, common prayer, and all their fellowship in service, may still be left to their loneliness. The final breakthrough to fellowship does not occur because, though they have fellowship with one another as believers and as devout people, they do not have fellowship as the undevout, as sinners. The pious fellowship permits no one to be a sinner. So everybody must conceal his sin from himself and from the fellowship. We dare not be sinners. Many Christians are unthinkably horrified when a real

sinner is suddenly discovered among the righteous. So we remain alone with our sin, living in lies and hypocrisy.[2]

We consign ourselves to plateaued growth in Christ if we yield to pride and fear and hide our sins. We grow as we own up to being real sinners, not theoretical sinners. All of us, as Christians, acknowledge generally that we are sinners. Rarer is the Christian who opens up to another about exactly *how* he or she is a sinner. But in this honesty, life blossoms.

Two Kinds of Dishonesty

There are two ways to be dishonest with fellow Christians: explicit dishonesty and implicit dishonesty. Explicit dishonesty is outright lying—telling someone you memorized all of Romans when you haven't memorized a single verse.

But there is also implicit dishonesty, which is much more subtle and also more common. This is the self-projection that gives an appearance of moral success when the truth is far different. Walking in the light is the alternate to the second of these. It is killing the preening and parading, the mask-wearing, the veneer, the keeping up of appearances. It is collapsing into transparency.

Everything in us resists this. Sometimes it feels like we would rather die. Actually, walking in the light is a certain kind of death. It feels as if our whole personhood, our self, is going into meltdown. We are losing our impressive appearance in front of another Christian. "In the confession of concrete sins the old man dies a painful, shameful death before the eyes of a brother," wrote Bonhoeffer.[3] But what

---

2 Dietrich Bonhoeffer, *Life Together*, trans. J. W. Doberstein (New York: HarperCollins, 1954), 110.
3 Bonhoeffer, *Life Together*, 114.

would you say to a baby terrified of being born, wanting to stay in the warmth and darkness of the womb, refusing to come out into the light? You would say: *If you stay in there, you will die. The way into life and growth is to come out into the light.*

Some of us are worn out with our Christian life, tired and discouraged, empty and running on fumes. Despite having in place a strong gospel theology, we are sputtering along, not really growing. Might it be because we have never climbed into 1 John 1:7? Are we trying to develop spiritually in the dark? Is there someone in your life who knows you are a sinner not only generally but also specifically? Not just in the abstract but also in the concrete? It is scary to go there with another brother or sister. But surgery is scary too. Yet is it not worth going through with it, given the healing and restoration and life and health awaiting us on the other side?

Objections

At this point some questions may be bubbling up.

Don't we have to confess our sins only to God? Nowhere in this text are we explicitly told to confess our sins to each other. Other places in the Bible say it explicitly: "Confess your sins to one another" (James 5:16). The only place we're told to "confess" in 1 John 1 is verse 9, which sounds like confession to God, not others: "If we confess our sins, he is faithful and just to forgive us our sins and to cleanse us from all unrighteousness."

Certainly, 1 John 1 includes confessing to God. That is fundamental. He is the one with whom we are dealing most deeply. But there is no way to make sense of the whole flow of this passage and the language of inter-personality unless walking in the light is also a horizontal matter. Verse 7 does not say, "But if we walk in the light, as he is in the light, the blood of Jesus his Son cleanses us from all sin." It says: "But if we walk in the light, as he is in the light, *we have fellowship with one another*, and the blood of Jesus his Son cleanses us from all sin." Walking in the light breeds depth of communion with fellow Christians.

Another question might be this: Is 1 John 1:7 saying I need to move through my life airing all my dirty laundry to every fellow Christian I come across?

No, certainly not. That would be self-focused and *un*loving, not to mention exhausting and awkward. This text is leading us not into exhaustive vulnerability but into redemptive vulnerability. But surely for most of us, the greater difficulty is under-confessing our sins to one another rather than over-confessing them. It takes wisdom to do this well. And I certainly do not want to erect a new, subtle legalism by which we begin to believe that God withholds his own forgiveness of us until we get sufficiently honest with other believers. That would be works righteousness and the loss of the gospel itself. But what if each of us determined to find one person—someone of the same gender, to head off any possibility of unhealthy attachments—who knew who we really are, inside and out? No pretense, no games, nothing impressive or put on?

Another hindrance to what I'm saying might go something like this: *But, Dane, as soon as I confess my sins to another human, the clock starts ticking. And I can't live with that kind of pressure.*

Of course not. Who could? If we expect each other to begin healing immediately, as soon as something is out in the light, we kill the whole point of mutual confession. God does not extend forgiveness to us vertically with an attached timescale; why would we put a timescale on each other horizontally? Certainly, we want to feel the urgency of the need for growth; the joy and usefulness and very soul health of the sinner is at stake. But none of us grows through pressure. It is the very absence of pressure that creates a fertile environment for killing sin and growing.

Here's what happens when we begin to get honest, even with just one other person. The two circles of what we know ourselves to be and what we present ourselves to be overlap. Rather than the private Dane being one person and the public Dane a different person, there's just one Dane. We become whole. Integrated. Strong. But the keeping up of appearances is an exhausting way to live.

Honesty with each other has many powerful results. This verse mentions two:

1. We have fellowship with one another.
2. The blood of Jesus his Son cleanses us from all sin.

We'll take them in that order.

Fellowship with One Another

The hell of aloneness! We simply were made for nothing less than a one-another existence. Unbelievers can enjoy only a dim shadow of this reality, but for those of us in Christ, we have been swept into the glory of inter-personality, and we have a resource in the gospel to enjoy honesty of life with others. Categories such as introversion and extroversion, useful as they are, do not penetrate to the even deeper matter, the fundamental way in which God wired all of us, introverts and extroverts alike, for human fellowship. *Even introverts get lonely.*

We were made to be together, to speak to each other, to share our hearts, to laugh together, to co-enjoy a beautiful flower. The pain of a sorrow is doubled when endured alone but greatly lessened when borne by another alongside us; likewise the satisfaction of a joy is doubled when celebrated with another yet lessened when enjoyed alone.[4] We pant for a bonded spirit with others, for shared hearts, for togetherness. Often our idolatrous pursuits through sexual immorality, overindulgence in alcohol, or social media platform-building are all simply misplaced longings for human fellowship. If we traced those heart-eroding pursuits down to their source, we would find, among other things, simply an absence of real Christian fellowship.

And here is the picture that the New Testament and a passage such as 1 John 1 is giving us. Before us lies a main hall, prepared for feasting. The tables are piled high with all the dishes we could imagine. The chandeliers are bright, the flowers beautifully arranged. The chairs are comfortable and close together. Seating is unlimited; anyone can jump in. But off the hall are ten thousand little dark rooms with space for only one person each, where we all tend to lurk, hiding with our shames and sins and failures, terrified lest anyone should see our blemishes out in the light. And 1 John 1:7—"If we walk in the light, as he is in the light, we have fellowship with one another"—is inviting us to the feast. Together. We are being beckoned out into the joy of humility and honesty with each other, where we feast, where we are nourished, where we are no longer alone.

As we walk in the light with each other, the walls come crashing down. We relax into a new way of being, a liberated way of existing with one another. Fellowship ignites and burns brightly. We are actually able to enjoy others, instead of just using them or constantly being in impress mode. Indeed, keeping up appearances has become so normal to us, we don't even realize how deeply we're mired in it. Surely one of the shocks of the new earth, when all our fallenness and sin and self-concern have evaporated, will be the startling new

---

4   Drew Hunter helped me to see this through his book *Made for Friendship: The Relationship That Halves Our Sorrows and Doubles Our Joys* (Wheaton, IL: Crossway, 2018).

freedom and pleasure of simply being around other people. Emptied of any need to present ourselves a certain way, we will have finally come truly alive. We will be free.

The message of the New Testament is that we can begin to enjoy that freedom—not perfectly, but truly—now. Which brings us to the second result of walking in the light.

Cleansing from All Sin

"The blood of Jesus his Son cleanses us from all sin." This little statement tucked into the back end of 1 John 1:7 is the whole reason any one of us will ever make it to heaven one day. We are cleansed by the blood of Christ.

This reality ties in to my earlier emphases on the love of Christ (chap. 4) and the doctrine of justification (chap. 5). The category of "cleansing," however, makes its own contribution. In the gospel we are united to Christ not because of any loveliness in us but only because of his own capacious loving heart. And many blessings flow from this: we are judged in the right and freed to leave the courtroom (justified), we are welcomed fully into the family of God (adopted), we are restored to a friendly relationship with the Father (reconciled), and so on. We are also, according to 1 John 1:7, made clean. We are given a bath. A one-time, permanently effective, cascading cleansing.

I think of mud wrestling at Camp Ridgecrest in the mountains of western North Carolina in the summer of 2000 as a camp counselor. After we were all caked with mud and exhausted, we got clean by jumping off the diving board into the lake. It felt great to submerge, feel the mud all wash off, and come up for air clean once more. We could have tried picking and rubbing with our hands, but we'd never get as clean that way—and anyway, our hands too were dirty, so we'd be trying to get the dirt off with more dirt. The gospel works the same way. We can never scrape ourselves clean. But if we are plunged into the lake of divine cleansing, we come up clean, and unlike the cleansing of that North Carolina lake, this cleansing means we can never be dirtied again.

We'll keep sinning in lots of ways, of course, but what is most deeply true of us is that we have been decisively washed clean once and for all. How exactly does the blood of Christ cleanse us? That's a pretty strange concept when you ponder it—getting clean by someone else's blood. The broader teaching of Scripture makes clear that for fallen sinners, justice must be done if we are to be put right with our Creator once more. But in culminating fulfillment of the shed blood of the Passover lamb in the Old Testament law, Jesus stood in for his people and let his own blood be taken on their behalf. He offered his own life so that all who desire for Jesus's blood to stand in for the taking of their own blood can have that substitutionary transaction determine their own eternal destiny. In that way his blood cleanses us. It's either Jesus's blood or ours. Divine justice must be satisfied. And if his blood is shed on my behalf, the Father's wrath is satisfied and I get off scot-free. And one result of that, one way into an understanding of it, is *cleansing*. Jesus, the clean one, was treated as dirty so that I, the dirty one, am treated as clean.

Many of us feel irredeemably dirty. We know God loves us, and we believe we really are justified. We know heaven awaits us just around the next bend in the road. But in the meantime we can't get out from under the oppressive sense of dirtiness. Whether from abuse at the hand of others or our own sinful stupidities, we feel dirty. Beneath our sharp theology we feel disgusting. Our smiles and well-presented external appearance are at odds with what we find to be our deepest visceral experience.

The gospel answers that. If you are in Christ, heaven has bathed you. You have been rinsed clean and are now "un-dirty-able." It doesn't matter what you feel. That doesn't define you. Jesus was defiled to free you from your defiled status and your defiled feelings. That doesn't mean we will never battle feelings of defilement. But it does mean that one aspect of growing in Christ is bringing our subjective feelings of defilement into line with that objective, decisive, invincible, true-for-all-time-and-eternity cleansing in the blood of Christ. Notice that the text says we are cleansed "from *all* sin" (1 John 1:7). This is a comprehensive treatment.

It's not easy to believe we're clean. To take God at his word at this point is probably not far different from telling a man convinced he has a high fever, "You're healthy." But so it is. We must believe it, defying what we feel. Believe it audaciously. Believe in this cleansing with gospel defiance. As Luther said: "If as God's Son, Jesus shed His blood to redeem us and cleanse us from sin, and if we believe this, rubbing it under the devil's nose whenever he tries to plague and terrify us with our sins, the devil will soon be beaten; he will be forced to withdraw and to stop pestering us."[5]

Honesty Fuels Feeling Forgiven

A thoughtful reader may respond at this point: *The text says that "if we walk in the light . . . the blood of Jesus his Son cleanses us from all sin." Does that mean if we're not honest with each other, God won't cleanse us? Is this in fact turning the gospel itself on its head and making our status of clean dependent on something we do?*

---

5 Martin Luther, *Sermons on the Gospel of St. John 1–4*, in *Luther's Works*, ed. Jaroslav Pelikan and Helmut T. Lehmann, 55 vols. (Philadelphia: Fortress, 1955–1986), 22:24.

We know from the broader teaching of the Bible that this is not so. The text must mean that as we walk in the light—and only those swept into the mercies of the gospel and indwelt by the Spirit can begin to do this truly anyway—the cleansing blood of Christ becomes more real to us. It moves from believed theory to felt reality. We experience that forgiveness more deeply than we otherwise can. Our hearts crack open to receive it more deeply than before. The forgiveness of the gospel moves from printed recipe to mouthwatering experience. In other words, honesty with one another about our sinfulness is a pathway to what Luther, Lewis, and Schaeffer all testified to experiencing—fresh, liberating, more solid awareness of the gospel. No, honesty with others does not win us God's favor. But without honesty with others, we take a terrible risk and set ourselves up for our worse fall yet.

When you trust God enough to speak your sinfulness to another human, the channels of your heart are opened to feeling forgiven. This is because the same pride that stops us from confessing our sins to a brother or sister also hinders our felt belief in the gospel. Pride hinders fellowship both horizontally and vertically. Evading honesty before another Christian is more fundamentally a rejection of the gospel itself. Refusing to be honest with another is works righteousness in disguise; we are believing that we need to save face, to retain uprightness of appearance. But in conversion to Christianity we have already acknowledged that we are hopelessly sinful, with nothing to contribute but our need. The gospel says we have nothing within us to commend us to God; why would we leave that theology in Christian fellowship and pretend that we do have virtue within to commend us? We must be consistent. Put another way: At conversion, the old man died once and for all (Rom. 6:1–14; Eph. 4:20–24; Col. 3:1–4, 9–10). When we refuse to be honest in the presence of a fellow believer, we are bringing that old man back to life. We are returning to our pre-regenerate way of operating.[6]

Collapse into Flourishing

Do you want joy? John did say, after all, that he was writing 1 John "so that our joy may be complete" (1:4). Do you want to grow? Perhaps just on the other side of real honesty with another Christian there awaits you a depth of "fellowship . . . with the Father and with his Son Jesus Christ" (1:3) that will make what you presently believe seem, in comparison, utterly unreal.

Believe the gospel. Find a trustworthy friend. Bring that brother or sister into your fallenness in a redemptive but humiliatingly transparent way. Humble yourself down into the death of honesty and see what life blossoms on the other side. Find yourself feeling bathed afresh in the gospel of grace. And as you dare to go deeper into honesty and deeper into the experience of the cleansing blood of Christ, watch your heart relax into the growth you long for.

---

6 For further unpacking of this paragraph, see Bonhoeffer, *Life Together*, 114–15.

7

Pain

OUR NATURAL INSTINCTS TELL US that the way forward in the
Christian life is by avoiding pain so that, undistracted, we can get
down to the business at hand of growing in Christ. The New Testament tells us again and again, however, that pain is a means, not an
obstacle, to deepening in Christian maturity. The anguish, disap-
pointments, and futility that afflict us are themselves vital building
blocks to our growth. We are "heirs of God and fellow heirs with
Christ, provided we suffer with him in order that we may also be
glorified with him" (Rom. 8:17). We most deeply know Christ as
we "share his sufferings" (Phil. 3:10). "For the moment all discipline
seems painful rather than pleasant, but later it yields the peaceful fruit
of righteousness to those who have been trained by it" (Heb. 12:11).

Pain will foster growth like nothing else can—if we will let it.

The Universality of Pain

One clarification we need to make right away is that we all experience
pain. I say this because it is common in some quarters of the Western
church to speak and preach and write as if only in other corners of
the world do believers suffer pain.

It is certainly true that overt persecution is not a universal phenomenon. It is also manifestly the case that believers in other parts of the world (I write this from the West and as a Westerner) face all manner of diverse hardships that many of us do not—shortage of drinking water, social ostracism, governmental constraints on gathering publicly for corporate worship, poverty, poor health care, lack of sound biblical and theological resources, an abundance of prosperity theology wooing and deceiving fellow believers, and more.

But sometimes this note of relative circumstantial comfort in the West can be struck in a way that minimizes or obscures the pain all believers, unique to their own lives, endure. No Christian, no matter where he or she lives, is immune to the painful experiences of cancer, betrayal by fellow Christians, vocational disappointment, psychological disorders, emotional meltdowns, wayward children, abusive bosses, or a hundred other adversities.

But when I speak of the universality of pain, I also have in mind something else, something beneath all of these concrete examples of adversity. There is, for all of us living between the first two chapters of the Bible and the last two, a pervasive futility shot through everything—our minds, our hearts, our consciences, every thought and word and meeting and email and rising to another day—there's something hard to articulate that infects it all. A sense of loss, of frustration, of non-flourishing, of shutdown, of daily grinding aimlessness, of spinning our wheels, of constantly hitting a wall. The Bible speaks to this, telling us that the whole "creation was subjected to futility" (Rom. 8:20) and is "groaning" like a mother in childbirth (Rom. 8:22). We should be careful to understand that "the whole creation" (Rom. 8:22) does not mean the natural created order minus humans. We are included in that futility. The text goes on to say that we too "groan inwardly as we wait eagerly" for God to put all things right in the end (Rom. 8:23). We are like a beautiful car trying to get from point A to point B with an engine and interior parts under the hood all gunked up. We're not running as we should.

Misery and darkness and anguish and regret and shame and lament color all that we say, do, and think. The reality of nightmares shows that this pain and futility even reaches into our subconscious and our sleep. We can go *nowhere* to escape the futility and pain of life in this fallen world. This is true for all believers. For unbelievers too, of course—but for believers the pain is different, because we know and feel more deeply that pain is not the way God made the world and not how things should be. That's why Romans 8 connects our groaning with the presence of "the firstfruits of the Spirit" (v. 23). We believers have been spiritually resurrected but not yet bodily resurrected, and that dissonance heightens our awareness of the "not-right-ness" of our fallen little existence. And every culture endures the daily futilities of life in this fallen world—that foreboding sense of sheer absurdity shot through life that blankets us in fresh despair with each new morning.

Pain is not the islands of our lives but the ocean; disappointment or letdown is the stage on which all of life unfolds, not an occasional blip on an otherwise comfortable and smooth life.

And what I want to say in this chapter is that a crucial building block in our growth in grace is a humble openness to receiving the bitternesses of life as God's gentle way of drawing us out of the misery of self and more deeply into spiritual maturity. Through pain God is inviting us up into "mature manhood, to the measure of the stature of the fullness of Christ" (Eph. 4:13).

We should be careful and cautious in how we approach this subject, because we are dealing with a reality that is not mere theological abstraction. This chapter is like peeling back a bandage on an open wound and doing some uncomfortable poking and prodding. The first thing to do with those enduring a fresh pain in their lives is not to hand them a book or quote them a verse or provide a theological reminder. The Bible says "weep with those who weep" (Rom. 12:15), not "provide theological answers to those who weep." A word of theological explanation, even a true word of theological explanation, to individuals in raw pain exacerbates the pain. They don't need us facing them, speaking. They need us next to them, weeping. The fact that Romans 8:28 comes before Romans 12:15 in the Bible does not mean it should come first in our counseling and friendships.

Nevertheless, while there is a time to weep, there is also a time to think (Eccles. 3:1–8). Throughout the course of our discipleship to Christ we all need to build a deep and strong foundation of understanding how to process and even redeem the anguish of our lives. Without this foundation our growth in Christ will be severely limited. That's the point of this chapter.

Slicing Off Branches

Each of us is like an otherwise healthy vine that has the perverse inclination to entangle all its tendrils around a poisonous tree that appears nourishing but actually deadens us. We have been warned that embracing this tree will kill us. But we can't help ourselves. We wrap ourselves around it. There's only one resort for the loving gardener. He must slice us free. Lop off whole branches, even. He must cause us to pass through the pass of loss, the pain of being diminished, of being lessened, in order to free us.

The world and its fraudulent offerings are like that poisonous tree. And our heavenly Gardener loves us too much to let us continue to commit soul suicide by getting more and more deeply attached to the world. Through the pain of disappointment and frustration,

God weans us from the love of this world. It feels like we're being crippled, like we're dying. In point of fact, we are being freed from the counterfeit pleasures of the world.

In 1949 C. S. Lewis wrote to Warfield Firor, an American professor of surgery, and in refreshing honesty said:

It's all there in the New Testament. . . . 'Dying to the world'—'the world is crucified to me and I to the world.' And I find I haven't begun: at least not if it means (and can it mean less) a steady and progressive disentangling of all one's motives from the merely natural or this-worldly objects: like training a creeper to grow up one wall instead of another. I don't mean disentangling from things wrong in themselves, but, say, from the very pleasant evening which we hope to have over a ham tomorrow night, or from gratification at my literary success. It is not the things, nor even the pleasure in them, but the fact that in such pleasures my heart, or so much of my heart, lies.

Or to put it in a fantastic form—if a voice said to me (and one I couldn't disbelieve) 'you shall never see the face of God, never help to save a neighbor's soul, never be free from sin, but you shall live in perfect health till you are 100, very rich, and die the most famous man in the world, and pass into a twilight consciousness of a vaguely pleasant sort forever'—how much would it worry me? How much compared with another war? Or even with an announcement that I should have to have all my teeth out? You see? And what right have I to expect the Peace of God while I thus put my whole heart, at least all my strongest wishes, in the world which he has warned me against?

Well, thank God, we shall not be left to the world. All His terrible resources (but it is we who force Him to use them) will be brought against us to detach us from it—insecurity, war, poverty, pain, unpopularity, loneliness. We must be taught that this tent is not home.[1]

Lewis here exposes our hearts. We who are honest with ourselves recognize how intractably entwined the vines of our hearts are with this world. That's not to say we should refuse to enjoy the good things of the world—a favorite meal, a beautiful sunset, the intimate pleasures of a spouse, gratification at a job well done. To resist such pleasures absolutely is, according to the apostles, demonic (1 Tim. 4:1–5). Rather, we should acknowledge that our hearts will latch on to anything in this world short of God himself and will seek to draw strength from that created thing instead of the Creator and his love. The biblical category for this perverse inclination of our hearts to look to the things of this world to quench our soul thirst is *idolatry*. Idolatry, as I defined it in chapter 5, is the folly of asking a gift to be a giver. The Bible tells us to locate our supreme longings and thirstings in God himself. He alone can satisfy (Ps. 16:11), and he promises he will satisfy (Jer. 31:25).

The problem is that we cannot, out of our own resources, lift up our hearts' deepest hopes from the world and transplant them in God. We think we can. We try. But it's like a child going into heart surgery confident that he can fix his heart on his own. He needs a surgeon to tend to him and to bring all that medical expertise to bear on the operation.

We too need heart surgery. And we too need the resources of a physician, the divine physician, who not only has all the right expertise

---

1   C. S. Lewis, *The Collected Letters of C. S. Lewis*, vol. 3, *Narnia, Cambridge, and Joy, 1950–1963*, ed. Walter Hooper (San Francisco: HarperCollins, 2009), 1007–8.

but also has embraced us into his deepest heart and loves us with a love as expansive as his own being (Eph. 3:18–19).

The operation takes a lifetime and often hurts. But it's healing us.

Only Two Choices

In a book published in 1630, five years before his death, Richard Sibbes wrote:

> Suffering brings discouragements, because of our impatience. "Alas!" we lament, "I shall never get through such a trial." But if God brings us into the trial he will be with us in the trial, and at length bring us out, more refined. We shall lose nothing but dross (Zech. 13:9). From our own strength we cannot bear the least trouble, but by the Spirit's assistance we can bear the greatest. The Spirit will add his shoulders to help us to bear our infirmities. The Lord will give us his hand to heave us up (Ps. 37:24). . . . It yields us comfort in desolate conditions, that then Christ has a throne of mercy at our bedside and numbers our tears and our groans.[2]

When pain washes into our lives, we immediately, instinctively feel as if we are losing. Something is happening in the debit category. We are going backward. *This is bad*, we think. Understandably so. In the economy of the gospel, however, we are united to a Savior who was himself arrested, crucified, put in a grave, and left for dead, only to rise in a triumphant glory not possible apart from that death. *Pain seeds glory.* Don't you want heavenly glory to settle all over your little life? How does that happen? The apostle Peter tells us: "If you are insulted for the name of Christ, you are blessed, because the Spirit

---

2 Richard Sibbes, *The Bruised Reed* (Edinburgh: Banner of Truth, 1998), 54–55.

of glory and of God rests on you" (1 Pet. 4:14). When insults send us reeling backward, when life hurts, our eyes are being lifted off of the unstable things of the world onto the stable God of the Bible. We are being given back our true selves. We are being beckoned, as Lewis put it, "further up and further in."[3] When pain comes, it is not simply to hurt us, to teach us a lesson, to whip us into shape; it is from a tender Father, for our healing. "You lie too near his heart for him to hurt you," wrote the Puritan John Flavel.[4]

When life hurts, we immediately find ourselves at an internal fork in the road. Either we take the road of cynicism, withdrawing from openheartedness with God and others, retreating into the felt safety of holding back our desires and longings, lest they get hurt again, or we press into greater depth with God than we have ever known. Either we smirk at what we said we believed about God's sovereignty and goodness, thinking that what we believed has just been disproven, or we put even more weight on our theology. The two circles of professed theology and heart theology, to that point distinct, are forced either to move farther away than ever or to perfectly overlap. Either we put all our weight on our theology, or we let our hearts calcify and harden. Either we let the divine physician continue the operation, or we insist on being wheeled out of the operating room. But pain does not let us go on as before.

Richard Davis was a pastor in England during the age of the Puritans. At one point he sought out the great John Owen for spiritual counsel. Sinclair Ferguson recounts what happened:

---

3   This is the title of chap. 15 of C. S. Lewis, *The Last Battle* (San Francisco: HarperCollins, 1984).

4   John Flavel, *Keeping the Heart: How to Maintain Your Love for God* (Fearn, Ross-shire, Scotland: Christian Focus, 2012), 43.

In the course of conversation, Owen asked him, "Young man, pray in what manner do you go to God?"

"Through the Mediator, sir," answered Davis.

"That is easily said," replied Owen, "but I assure you it is another thing to go to God through the Mediator than many who make use of the expression are aware of. I myself preached Christ some years, when I had but very little, if any, experimental acquaintance with access to God through Christ; until the Lord was pleased to visit me with sore affliction, whereby I was brought to the mouth of the grave, and under which my soul was oppressed with horror and darkness; but God graciously relieved my spirit through a powerful application of Ps 130.4, *But there is forgiveness with thee that thou mayest be feared*, from whence I received special instruction, peace, and comfort, in drawing near to God through the Mediator, and preached thereupon immediately after my recovery."[5]

Notice the words "with sore affliction." It was through, not in avoidance of, a painful trial that assurance of forgiveness came home to Owen. He had preached the gospel for years, but only through this trial did the gospel he had preached move from professed theology to heart theology. The two circles overlapped.

If you want to be a solid, weighty, radiant old man or woman someday, let the pain in your life force you to believe your own theology. Let it propel you into deeper fellowship with Christ than ever before. Don't let your heart dry up. He is in your pain. He is refining you. All that you will lose, Sibbes reminds us, is the dross of Self and misery that in your deepest heart you want to shed anyway.

---

5 Sinclair B. Ferguson, *John Owen on the Christian Life* (Edinburgh: Banner of Truth, 1987), 100n1. Ps. 130 became so personally precious to Owen that he would go on to write a dense 200-page exposition of it, found in vol. 6 of his collected works.

God loves us too much to let us remain shallow. How frothy and facile we would be if we lived all of life without pain.

Your tears are his tools.

Tears and Joy

While we're talking about tears, perhaps it would be worth reflecting briefly on their salutary effect in our lives. Our tears do not hinder growth. Our tears accelerate and deepen growth. That isn't always true, of course. We can let our tears sour us rather than sweeten us. But tears often simply reflect the removal of distraction. We are finally getting in touch with reality and with ourselves. We see more who we really are, in all our vileness. We see more deeply who Jesus Christ is, in all his tenderness.

Do you not find, as you reflect back on your life, that there were times when, sitting alone in your tears, you experienced a sublime depth of joy, of reality with God, that no stand-up comedian could give you? If someone had walked in on you at one such moment and seen your tear-streamed face, they would immediately have concluded you were in distress. But they would have misinterpreted what was going on. Looking up and seeing your interrupter, you might have been tempted to sweep away the awkwardness with a quick joke, but that would have caused your welling joy to immediately dissipate.

The Bible says,

> Sorrow is better than laughter,
> for by sadness of face the heart is made glad. (Eccles. 7:3)

This statement in Ecclesiastes is not meant to be absolute; remember that this is Hebrew wisdom literature, and it requires a certain care in seeing its meaning. But it is saying *something*. And the point of a text like this is that the solemnity of tears deepens us into a certain kind of solidity and robustness of personhood that gets beneath the froth informing so much of our interactions with others and even our solitary self-reflection.

The Bible also says the opposite: "Even in laughter the heart may ache" (Prov. 14:13). According to Proverbs 14, a smiling exterior can often veil an aching interior; according to Ecclesiastes 7, a weeping exterior can often adorn quiet, deep, solid joy.

Let yourself cry as you grow. Don't stuff your emotions down. Growing in Christ isn't all smiles and laughter. Let your tears, and the wounds they reflect, take you deeper with Christ than you could ever otherwise go. As I've heard my dad say, "Deep wounds deepen us."

Mortification

So far in this chapter we've been talking about the kind of pain that comes to us without our permission—suffering, anguish, frustration, washing into our lives contrary to what we want or expect. But alongside this kind of pain in which we are passive is another kind of pain in which we are active. I refer to the age-old discipline that theologians call mortification.

Mortification is just a theological word for "putting to death." It refers to the duty of every Christian to kill sin. As Owen put it in the most important work ever written on killing sin, "Be killing sin or sin will be killing you."[6] None of us is ever in neutral. Right now, every one of us who is in Christ is either killing sin or being killed by sin. Either getting stronger or getting weaker. If you think you're coasting, you're actually going backward. There's no cruise-control spiritually. It may feel as if you're currently in neutral, but our hearts

6 John Owen, *Overcoming Sin and Temptation*, ed. Kelly M. Kapic and Justin Taylor (Wheaton, IL: Crossway, 2006), 50.

are like gardens: if we aren't proactively rooting out the weeds, the weeds are growing, even if we don't notice.

The work of mortification is for every Christian. Theologians have long spoken of mortification as working in tandem with vivification—there's putting to death, and there's being made alive. At conversion we "die" once and for all and are made alive once and for all. But there is also the daily pattern of going down into death and up into life.

This teaching on mortification is the most *active* facet of our growing in Christ. The other chapters of this book focus primarily on what we receive in the gospel. And that is as it should be. Christian salvation and the growth that it ignites is fundamentally a matter of grace, rescue, help, deliverance—it is God invading our miserable little lives and triumphing gloriously and persistently over all the sin and self he finds there. But that does not mean we are robots. The verse on which John Owen based his book on mortification was Romans 8:13: "For if you live according to the flesh you will die, but if by the Spirit you put to death [i.e., mortify] the deeds of the body, you will live." One of the key points Owen lingers over in his book is captured by the three words "by the Spirit." We do not kill sin through the resources inherent to us. We will come back to the Holy Spirit in the last chapter of this book. But we note now that even the most active aspect of our sanctification, the facet where our own will is most thoroughly engaged, the mortification of our sin, is not something we tackle on our own. We do it "by the Spirit."

As we find ourselves being pulled down by sin and temptation, we cry out to the Spirit for grace and help, and then we act in conscious dependence on that Spirit, taking it by faith that we are, thanks to the Spirit, able to kill that sin or resist that temptation. The devil wants us to think we are impotent. But if God the Spirit is within us, the very power that raised Jesus's dead body to triumphant life is able to exert that same vital power in our little lives. As Paul said shortly before Romans 8:13: "If the Spirit of him who raised Jesus from the dead dwells in you, he who raised Christ Jesus from the dead will also give life to your mortal bodies through his Spirit who dwells in you" (Rom. 8:11).

Mortification versus Self-Flagellation

We need to get a possible misconception out onto the table before proceeding. In speaking of pain as a vital ingredient to our growth, and especially now as we speak of our self-inflicted "pain" of mortification, we must be ever vigilant not to view the pain of our lives as contributing in any way to Christ's atoning work. That may sound obvious, but the temptation to do so is subtle and insidious. We must remember what we rehearsed in chapter 5 about acquittal. In the finished work of Christ on the cross we are completely liberated from the accusing powers of the devil and our own consciences. In killing sin we are not completing Christ's finished work; we are responding to it. Christ was killed so that our own relative success or failure in killing sin is no part of the formula of our adoption into God's family.

In Holy Week of 2009 the *Boston Globe* ran a story with images of various Christian communities around the world celebrating Maundy Thursday.[7] One particularly arresting image was from the city of San Fernando in the Philippines, where several Roman Catholic penitents were photographed as they knelt before a church, shirts off and backs bloodied, flagellating themselves in an attempt to atone for their sins. We are rightly horrified by such an image, knowing that the need for

---

7 "The Big Picture: News Stories in Photographs," Boston.com, April 10, 2009, http://archive
   .boston.com/bigpicture/2009/04/holy_week.html.

this kind of self-inflicted pain has been wonderfully eradicated by Christ's own suffering. It would be an odd response for a criminal, bailed out of prison, to promptly go down to county hall to pay the bail fee himself; he's already been freed.

But I wonder if we really take to heart what is wrong about such a practice. Is it not a constant temptation for Western Christians to engage in such self-flagellation psychologically and emotionally, if not physically? What's your response when you are aware of your sin? If you're like me, you know Christ died for that, and you're grateful. But just to show how grateful you are, or to seal the deal, you do a bit of psychological self-inflicted pain to top it off. Not, of course, to self-consciously add to Christ's work. Heaven forbid. Just to let him know how much you care, to make it clear that you're a *serious* Christian. Nothing physical. Just a bit of extra externalized obedience or formal service or sucking on the guilt.

The trouble is that the whole message of the Bible is that if we're going to add a cherry of self-contribution on top of Christ's work to really be okay, we have to provide the whole sundae. All or nothing. And the tragedy is that though we assent theologically to the truth that we can't add to Christ's work, we try to put ourselves emotionally at ease by helping the Lord out a bit. Yet adding something to seal the deal is precisely what will create uneasiness about whether the deal ever really is sealed. What if we don't seal the deal well enough?

That innate instinct to help out God's opinion of us by self-medicated doses of humanly generated recompense seems so sensible. So reasonable. Intuitive. How else would we live? But the glory of the gospel is that this attempt to help God out is not only unnecessary but a rejection of God's offer in Christ. It isn't a strengthening of God's opinion of me but a dilution of it. It doesn't honor Christ's sacrificial work on our behalf; it dishonors his work. And it will make us grouchy and tense instead of humble and free.

As we reflect on mortifying our sin, then, we do so mindful that we can never strengthen the objective declaration of "acquitted and righteous" that is ours by faith alone on the basis of the finished work of Christ alone.

Suffocating Sin

That's what mortification *isn't*. It isn't adding to Christ's atoning work. What, positively, is it?

We don't mainly mortify sin by looking at it. We have to be aware of it, of course. But we don't kill sin the way a soldier kills an enemy in battle, by zeroing in on the enemy himself. Killing sin is a strange battle because it happens by *looking away from the sin*. By "looking away" I don't mean emptying our minds and trying to create a mental vacuum. I mean looking at Jesus Christ. In the same way that playing matchbox cars on the front lawn loses its attractiveness when we're invited to spend the afternoon at a NASCAR race, sin loses its appeal as we allow ourselves to be re-enchanted time and again with the unsurpassable beauty of Jesus. Remember what we noted in chapter 1 about "the unsearchable riches of Christ" (Eph. 3:8). Sin feels like riches, but it is counterfeit riches, and one very quickly hits bottom on its pleasures. It doesn't deliver. Christ, on the other hand, is real riches, and one never hits bottom on them. They are unsearchable.

We feed sin by coddling it, pining after it, daydreaming about it, giving vent to it. We suffocate sin by redirecting our gaze to Christ. When I say "redirecting our gaze," I mean looking on him with "the eyes of your hearts" (Eph. 1:18). It's a little odd for the Bible to speak of a body part itself having body parts—how does a heart have eyes? But remember that in the Bible the "heart" is the animating center of all we do, the deepest part of us, and the spring of our deepest motives and longings. Scripture is showing us that what we give our hearts to—what we love and desire—determines our spiritual health. If we have rock-solid theology and wide-ranging behavioral conformity to God's commands and stellar church attendance but our hearts are flowing against all that and are actually pursuing notoriety or swelling bank accounts or anything else, we will never make headway mortifying sin. How could we? If our hearts' deepest loyalties belong to anything other than God, we're simply playing games to act as if we're out to mortify sin. Why would we try to kill what we love?

But when our hearts redirect their gaze to the Jesus of the Bible in all his glorious gentleness and dazzling love, sin gets starved and begins to wilt. As we enjoy the truths this book has been reflecting on—realities such as our union with Christ and his unshakable embrace of us and God's irreversible acquittal of us—then, right then, spiritual life and vigor begin to have the ascendancy, and the grip of sin loosens. Flavel puts it this way: "Would you have your corruptions mortified? This is the way: to have the food and fuel removed that maintained them; for as prosperity begat and fed them, so adversity, when sanctified, is a means to kill them."[8]

There is no special technique to mortifying sin. You simply open your Bible and let God surprise you each day with the wonder of his love, proven in Christ and experienced in the Spirit.

Fighting Is Winning

We have to end this chapter on a note of hope. "It is the sin of upright persons sometimes," says Flavel, "to exercise an unreasonable

8 Flavel, *Keeping the Heart*, 45.

severity against themselves."[9] He goes on to reassure his readers that while they may look inside themselves and see all kinds of filth and plenty of unbelief and a variety of disordered loves, yet seeing also a spark of desire for God, a glimmer of longing for Christ, may put them at ease.

Best of all, they should stop looking within themselves at all and look out to Christ. In any case, his point is that the struggle itself reflects life. If we were not regenerate, we simply wouldn't care. The longing for Christ, the frustration at our falls, the desire to be fully yielded to God—these are the cries of life, even if immature life. God will not let you go. He will be sure to love you on into heaven.

In the meantime, he is teaching you not to give up your mortification project. Your very efforts to fight your sin distress Satan. Fighting is winning. C. S. Lewis put it well in a January 1942 letter, and with this word of comfort we close this chapter:

> I know all about the despair of overcoming chronic temptations.
>
> It is not serious provided self-offended petulance, annoyance at breaking records, impatience etc doesn't get the upper hand. *No amount* of falls will really undo us if we keep on picking ourselves up each time. We shall of course be very muddy and tattered children by the time we reach home. But the bathrooms are all ready, the towels put out, and the clean clothes are airing in the cupboard.
>
> The only fatal thing is to lose one's temper and give it up. It is when we notice the dirt that God is most present to us: it is the very sign of His presence.[10]

---

9   Flavel, *Keeping the Heart*, 94.
10 Lewis, *Collected Letters*, 3:507; emphasis original.

8

Breathing

ALL THE CHAPTERS OF THIS BOOK till now have reflected on overarching themes. Realities such as union with Christ, or the embrace of Christ, or acquittal before God through the wonder of justification—these are timeless truths we spend a lifetime believing and absorbing into our hearts. But how, practically, day by day, do we do that? What are the actual tools by which that belief and heart absorption take place?

This chapter answers that question. In truth there are many valid answers to the question—the importance of regularly partaking of the sacraments of the church, and being part of Christian fellowship through the local church, and cultivating deep Christian friendships, and so on. But I want to consider just two ordinary, predictable, wondrous, vital practices: Bible reading and prayer.

And the way to think about these two practices is by the metaphor of breathing. Reading the Bible is inhaling. Praying is exhaling.

Our Greatest Earthly Treasure

What is the Bible? It is your greatest earthly treasure. You will stand in strength, and grow in Christ, and walk in joy, and bless this world no further than you know this book. Here's the introduction to the Bibles published by the Gideons:

> The Bible contains the mind of God, the state of man, the way of salvation, the doom of sinners, and the happiness of believers. Its doctrines are holy, its precepts are binding, its histories are true, and its decisions are immutable. Read it to be wise, believe it to be safe, and practice it to be holy. It contains light to direct you, food to support you, and comfort to cheer you.
>
> It is the traveler's map, the pilgrim's staff, the pilot's compass, the soldier's sword, and the Christian's charter. Here Paradise is restored, Heaven opened and the gates of Hell disclosed.
>
> Christ is its grand subject, our good its design, and the glory of God its end. It should fill the memory, rule the heart, and guide the feet. Read it slowly, frequently, and prayerfully. It is a mine of wealth, a paradise of glory, and a river of pleasure. It is given you in life, will be opened at the judgment, and be remembered forever.
>
> It involves the highest responsibility, rewards the greatest labor, and will condemn all who trifle with its sacred contents.

I quote this in full because these reverent words bring us unavoidably face-to-face with the sacred preciousness of the Bible. Who can read this and not want to give his or her whole life to being a student of the Bible? Scripture is not an ancillary benefit for a life otherwise well ordered, in need of a little extra boost. Scripture is shaping and fueling and oxygenating. It is vital. Jesus prayed, "Sanctify them in the truth; your word is truth" (John 17:17). *Deeper* is a book on sanctification. And Jesus said we need the word of God, which is truth, for that to happen.

Reconstructing

How so?

Fallen human beings enter this world *wrong*. We do not look at ourselves correctly, we do not view God correctly, we do not understand the way to be truly happy, we are ignorant of where all human history is heading, and we do not have the wisdom that makes life work well. And so on. The Christian life—our growth in Christ—is nothing other than the lifelong deconstruction of what we naturally think and assume and the reconstruction of truth through the Bible. Picture a building that has been erected by untrained construction workers and thus is a complete disaster—floors unlevel, windows the wrong size, paint colors that clash, roof shingles missing, and even the foundation off-kilter. That's us. And the Bible is the all-in-one, universal, industrial-strength tool by which the divine Architect puts us back together the way we were meant to be.

We tend to think we are put on this earth to make a name for ourselves. The Bible dismantles that notion and replaces it with the knowledge that we are put here to spread God's reputation and honor. We tend to think God will accept us if we meet a minimum bar of personal goodness. The Bible dismantles that and insists that God accepts us when we lay down the attempt to offer God anything of our own and instead receive his favor based on the work of his own Son. We tend to think we're not worth much and are insignificant in the big scheme of things. The Bible dismantles that and tells us we are made in God's own image with inherent dignity and that we were made to rule the cosmos in eternal glory. We tend to think the things of this world such as food, sex, and long vacations satisfy our souls. The Bible dismantles that and teaches us that the gifts can never quench our soul thirst; only the giver can do that.

And so on. The Bible reeducates us. The Bible makes sages out of fools. It corrects us.

Oxygen

But we need to press deeper. The Bible not only corrects us; it also oxygenates us. We need a Bible not only because we are wrong in our minds but also because we are empty in our souls.

This is why I like the metaphor of breathing. Taking a big breath into our lungs fills us with fresh air, gives us oxygen, calms us down, provides focus, and brings mental clarity. What inhaling does for us physically, Bible reading does for us spiritually.

In this shifty, uncertain world, God has given us actual words. Concrete, unmoving, fixed words. We can go to the rock of Scripture amid the shifting sands of this life. Your Bible is going to have the same words tomorrow that it does today. Friends can't provide that—they will move in and out of your life, loyal today but absent tomorrow. Parents and their counsel will die. Your pastor will not always be available to take your call. The counselor who has given you such sage instruction will one day retire, or maybe you'll move out of state. But you can roll out of bed tomorrow morning and, whatever stressors slide uncomfortably across your mental horizon as you groan with the anxieties of the day, your friend the Bible is unfailingly steady. It lies there, awaiting opening, eager to steady you amid all the unanswered questions before you that day. It will give you what you need and not evade you. Our truest wisdom and only safety is to build our lives on its words (Matt. 7:24–27).

In fact, we should not be saying "it" but "he." Through Scripture God himself addresses us. The reason the Bible does not shift and move is that God does not shift and move. Your Bible is not just the best book there is among all the books out there. The Bible is a different *kind* of book. It's of another class. It is similar to other books in that it is bound between two covers and is filled with small black letters comprising words throughout. But the Bible is different from other books in the way rainfall is different from your garden hose—it comes from above and provides a kind of nourishment far beyond what our own resources can provide.

Why? Because the Bible's author is God, and God knows exactly what will nourish us. Yes, human authors wrote the actual books of the Bible. But they "spoke from God as they were carried along by the Holy Spirit" (2 Pet. 1:21). Did God or humans write the Bible? Both—in that order. God told Jeremiah, "Behold, I have put my words in your mouth" (Jer. 1:9). That's precisely the way to understand Scripture: God put his words in human mouths. The words are truly God's, but he gave them through the distinct personalities and word banks of the human authors. This is why the simple elegance of John can differ markedly from the terse earthiness of Mark or the flowery, lengthy sentences of Paul, while all three are truly and fully speaking God's own words.

And because the Bible was written in other languages—Hebrew, Aramaic, and Greek—we will be maximally nourished by Scripture to the degree that we are reading a translation of the Bible that shows what the original wording, with maximal transparency but with readable and dignified English, is. The English Standard Version, in my opinion, is the single best translation available today to that end. And any Christian who will take the time to learn something of the original languages will profit tenfold from whatever energy is expended. The health of the church depends on knowledge of the original languages, and pastors and church leaders should call their people—any who are so inclined—to learn the languages alongside them.[1]

A Book of Good News

Many of us approach the Bible not as oxygenating, however, but as suffocating. We see the Bible lying there on the end table. We know we should open it. Sometimes we do. But it is usually with a sense of begrudged duty. Life is demanding enough, we think. Do I really need more demands? Do I have to hear even more instruction telling me how to live?

That's an understandable feeling. But it is lamentably wrong. And it brings me to the central thing I want to say about the Bible as we continue to think about how real sinners get traction for real change in their lives. The Bible is good news, not a pep talk. *News.* What is news? It is reporting on something that has happened. The Bible is like the front page of the newspaper, not the advice column. To be sure, the Bible also has plenty of instruction. But the exhortations and commands of Scripture flow out of the Bible's central message, like ribs flowing out of a spine or sparks from a fire or rules of the house for the kids. Paul said that the Old Testament was written so that "through the encouragement of the Scriptures we might have hope" (Rom. 15:4). He said, "The sacred writings . . . are able to make you wise for salvation through faith in Christ Jesus" (2 Tim. 3:15). The Bible is help, not oppression. It is given to buoy us along in life, not drag us down. Our own dark thoughts of God are what cause us to shrink back from opening and yielding to it.

---

1 An excellent introduction to the importance of learning the biblical languages is Dirk Jongkind, *An Introduction to the Greek New Testament Produced at Tyndale House, Cambridge* (Wheaton, IL: Crossway, 2019).

When we yawn over the Bible, that's like a severe asthmatic yawning over the free offer of a ventilator while gasping for air. Read the Bible asking not *mainly* whom to imitate and how to live but what it shows us about a God who loves to save and about sinners who need saving. In other words, the earlier chapters of this book outlining Jesus and union with Christ and justification and the love of God—each of these chapters is itself one way into the central message of the Bible.

Perhaps it seems obvious that the Bible is good news. How else would we read it? Here are nine common but wrong ways to read the Bible:

1. *The warm-fuzzies approach*—reading the Bible for a glowing, subjective experience of God, ignited by the words of the text, whether we understand what they actually *mean* or not. Result: frothy reading.

2. *The grumpy approach*—reading the Bible out of nothing but a vague sense that we're supposed to, to get God off our backs for the day. Result: resentful reading.

3. *The gold-mine approach*—reading the Bible as a vast, cavernous, dark mine, in which one occasionally stumbles upon a nugget of inspiration. Result: confused reading.

4. *The hero approach*—reading the Bible as a moral hall of fame that gives us one example after another of heroic spiritual giants to emulate. Result: despairing reading.

5. *The rules approach*—reading the Bible on the lookout for commands to obey to subtly reinforce a sense of personal superiority. Result: Pharisaical reading.

6. *The Indiana Jones approach*—reading the Bible as an ancient document about events in the Middle East a few thousand years ago that are irrelevant to my life today. Result: bored reading.

7. *The magic-eight-ball approach*—reading the Bible as a road map
   to tell me where to work, whom to marry, and what car to buy.
   Result: anxious reading.

8. *The Aesop's Fables approach*—reading the Bible as a loose collec
   tion of nice stories strung together independently, each with a
   nice moral at end. Result: disconnected reading.

9. *The doctrine approach*—reading the Bible as a theological reposi-
   tory to plunder for ammunition for our next theology debate at
   Starbucks. Result: cold reading.

There is some truth to each of these approaches. But to make any
of them the dominant lens through which we read Scripture is to
turn the Bible into a book it was never intended to be. The right way
to read the Bible is the *gospel approach*. This means we read every
passage as somehow contributing to the single, overarching storyline
of Scripture, which culminates in Jesus.

Just as you wouldn't parachute into the middle of a novel, read a
paragraph out of context, and expect to understand all that it means,
you cannot expect to understand all that a passage of Scripture means
without plotting it in the big arc of the Bible's narrative. And the
main story of the Bible is that God sent his Son, Jesus, to do what
Adam and Israel and we ourselves have failed to do—honor God and
obey him fully. Every word in the Bible contributes to that message.
Jesus himself said so. In a theology debate with the religious elite of
the day, Jesus told those who claimed to be faithful to Moses and
thus opposed to Christ, "If you believed Moses, you would believe
me; for *he wrote of me*" (John 5:46). Jesus told his disciples, "Everything written *about me* in the Law of Moses and the Prophets and
the Psalms"—shorthand for the entire Old Testament—"must be
fulfilled" (Luke 24:44).

The Bible is good news. It must be read as gospel. And the result of this approach is transforming reading. We grow. As Luther said:

> He who would correctly and profitably read Scripture should see to it that he finds Christ in it; then he finds life eternal without fail. On the other hand, if I do not so study and understand Moses and the prophets as to find that Christ came from heaven for the sake of my salvation, became man, suffered, died, was buried, rose, and ascended into heaven so that through him I enjoy reconciliation with God, forgiveness of all my sins, grace, righteousness, and life eternal, then my reading in Scripture is of no help whatsoever to my salvation.
>
> I may, of course, become a learned man by reading and studying Scripture and preach what I have acquired; yet all this would do me no good whatever.[2]

The Defining Habit

So as you seek to grow in Christ by becoming a deeper human, accept and embrace the truth that you will go deeper with Christ no further than you go into Scripture. To read Scripture is to read of Christ. To read it is to hear his voice. And to hear his voice of comfort and counsel is to hear an invitation to become the human being God has destined you to be.

So build Bible reading into your life in the very same way you build breakfast into your life. After all, we humans are habit-forming creatures. Our morning coffee, our evening dessert, the way we care for our vehicles, our methods for decompressing such as jogging or

2 Martin Luther, *Sermons I*, in *Luther's Works*, ed. Jaroslav Pelikan and Helmut T. Lehmann, 55 vols. (Philadelphia: Fortress, 1955–1986), 51:4.

movies or bird-watching—and all our habits reflect an acquired taste, over a long period of time, resulting in daily rituals without which we do not feel we have lived a normal day. And I want to say: *Make the Bible your central daily ritual.* Make it your habit without which you have not lived a normal day. By no means allow this to become a law towering over and condemning you. God's favor does not take a hit when you fail to read the Bible some days. But consider yourself undernourished if skipping that spiritual meal becomes normal. Fight to stay healthy. Stay hooked up to the IV of gospel and help and counsel and promise by reading the Bible each day. Draw life and strength from the Scriptures.

To switch back to our original metaphor: take your asthmatic soul in one hand and the oxygen tank of the Bible in your other hand, and bring the two together. Reading the Bible is inhaling.

Exhaling

And praying is exhaling. Breathe in; breathe out. We take in the life-giving words of God, and we breathe them back out to God in prayer.

The reason I wanted to include both Scripture and prayer in a single chapter in this book on growing in Christ is to underscore how interrelated and mutually dependent they are. We can easily think of these two disciplines as independent activities. We read the Bible, and we pray. But the most effective way to pray is to turn your Bible reading into prayer.[3] And the best way to read the Bible is prayerfully.

How does prayer fit in to this book? This is a book on growing in Christ. And my resounding theme is that the Christian life is at heart a matter not of doing more or behaving better but of going

---

3 A really useful practical guide to this end is Donald S. Whitney, *Praying the Bible* (Wheaton, IL: Crossway, 2015).

deeper. And the primary emphasis I have wanted to give is that we grow specifically by going deeper into the gospel, into the love of Christ and our experienced union with him. As we now think about prayer, here is what we are doing: we are reflecting on the way our souls must go out to God in Christ to desire, to long for, to receive, to dwell in, to thank him for his endless love. The gospel comes to us in the Scriptures, and in prayer we receive and enjoy it.

Put differently, to connect prayer with Scripture reading is simply to acknowledge that God is a real person with whom believers have an actual, moment-by-moment relationship. The Bible is God's speaking to us; prayer is our speaking to him. If we do not pray, we do not believe God is an actual person. We may say we do. But we don't really. If we do not pray, we actually think he is an impersonal force of some kind, a kind of Platonic ideal, distant and removed, powerful but abstract. We don't view him as a *Father*.

Children Speaking to Dad

I never had to tell my kids to try to start speaking. Just as naturally as they began breathing when they were born, they began trying to speak when they were several months old. The impulse to speak was wired into them.

Likewise, children of God naturally find within themselves the impulse to speak to their heavenly Father. Romans and Galatians tell us of the babbling urge to speak to our Father that comes when we are indwelt by the Spirit: we cry out "Abba! Father!" (Rom. 8:15; Gal. 4:6). This is a cry of intimacy, of dependence; the cry of a child. We often do not know exactly what or how to pray. Jesus gave us the Lord's Prayer as one way to help. But another help is simply the Spirit bubbling up within, joined to a mind stored with Scripture, taking us up into heaven with the gurglings of an infant. Jesus told us what to pray; but when we don't know what to pray, "the Spirit himself intercedes for us with groanings too deep for words" (Rom. 8:26). We have been united to Christ by the Spirit, and God therefore lives within us—when we can't pray, in a sense, *God prays for us*—"the Spirit *himself* intercedes for us."

And so we move through our day praying. The Bible says, "Pray without ceasing" (1 Thess. 5:17). That may sound impossibly out of reach. How am I to eat, sleep, and talk with my friends if I'm supposed to be praying all the time? But that's not the point of this text—the point is simply to move through your life praying rather than *only* sectioning off a few minutes in the morning or evening for prayer. To be sure, planned times of focused prayer are indispensable. But if that is all we ever do—if our only prayer all day long is a segmented couple of minutes praying through a list of items—we do not know him as Father. We have not drunk down the realities reflected on earlier in this book—who Jesus Christ most deeply is and our vital union with him and so on.[4]

What would you say to a ten-year-old daughter who never spoke to her dad, never asked him for anything, never thanked him, never expressed love to him, despite his many expressions of love to her? You would conclude that she believed she had a father only in theory, not in actuality. You could only conclude that her father's love was not *real* to her.

Move through your day praying. Let God be your moment-by-moment Father. Hear his voice in Scripture in the morning, and turn that Scripture into prayer—and then let that time with him, that

---

4 The best book on prayer that I am aware of, and one that makes this point of going through your day praying in conscious awareness of your adopted status, is Paul E. Miller, *A Praying Life: Connecting with God in a Distracting World*, rev. ed. (Colorado Springs: NavPress, 2017).

back-and-forth communion, send you off into your day communing with him all day long.

The Bible's Prayer Book

As we think about prayer in the Christian life, we need to pause and reflect on the one book of the Bible that is itself a series of prayers: the book of Psalms. I have said that the Bible is God speaking to us. But the Psalms are the one book in the Bible addressed to God. In it God takes us by the hand and gives us words to speak back to him. The Psalms are prayers.

So I propose to you, as you grow in Christ, that you form the vital habit of making the book of Psalms your lifelong companion. Befriend the Psalms deeply. Never go too long without making them your own prayers. They give voice, sacred voice, to every circumstance, every emotion, every distress we walk through in this fallen wilderness of a world. More precisely, the Psalms train our hearts in a gospel direction. They bring us to the great, glorious, basic truths we love and confess—most centrally the cross of Christ, which forgives us and is our own pattern for life. John Calvin wrote:

> Although the Psalms are replete with all the precepts which serve to frame our life to every part of holiness, piety, and righteousness, yet they will principally teach and train us to bear the cross; and the bearing of the cross is a genuine proof of our obedience, since by doing this, we renounce the guidance of our own affections, and submit ourselves entirely to God, leaving Him to govern us and to dispose of our life according to His will, so that the afflictions which are the bitterest and most severe to our nature become sweet to us because they proceed from Him.

In one word, not only will we find here general commendations of the goodness of God which may teach people to repose themselves in Him alone, but we will also find that the free remission of sins, which alone reconciles God toward us and procures for us settled peace with Him, is so set forth and magnified, as that here there is nothing wanting which relates to the knowledge of eternal salvation.[5]

As you read the Psalms unhurriedly, meditatively, allowing them to give voice to your own heart's distresses, you will find yourself thinking, *These poets know me.* In fact, they know me better than I know myself. They see my sin more clearly than I do. And they see the surprising abundance of God's redemption more clearly than I do. In short, they take me deeper. And thus foster my growth in Christ.

Inhale, Exhale

In May 2020 the *Wall Street Journal* ran a piece by James Nestor entitled "The Healing Power of Proper Breathing." The caption under the headline read, "How we inhale and exhale has profound effects on our health."[6] That is all I want to say in this chapter, spiritually speaking.

You wouldn't try to go through life holding your breath. So don't go through life without Bible reading and praying. Let your soul breathe. Oxygenate with the Bible; and breathe out the CO_2 of prayer as you speak back to God your wonder, your worry, and your waiting. He is not a force, not an ideal, not a machine. He is a person. Keep

5 John Calvin, "Preface to the Commentary on the Psalms," in *John Calvin: Writings on Pastoral Piety*, ed. Elsie McKie (New York: Paulist, 2001), 58.

6 James Nestor, "The Healing Power of Proper Breathing," *Wall Street Journal* (website), May 21, 2020, https://www.wsj.com/articles/the-healing-power-of-proper-breathing-11590098696.

open the channel between your little life and heaven itself through the Bible and prayer.

As you do, you will grow. You won't feel it day to day. But you'll come to the end of your life a radiant, solid man or woman. And you will have left in your wake the aroma of heaven. You will have blessed the world. Your life will have mattered.

9

Supernaturalized

IN HER BOOK *THE TAPESTRY* Edith Schaeffer recounts a conversation prompted by a question put to her by her husband, Francis:

> "Edith, I wonder what would happen to most churches and Christian work if we awakened tomorrow, and everything concerning the reality and work of the Holy Spirit, and everything concerning prayer, were removed from the Bible. I don't mean just ignored, but actually cut out—disappeared. I wonder how much difference it would make?"
>
> We concluded it would not make much difference in many board meetings, committee meetings, decisions, and activities.[1]

The natural inertia of all our Christian ministry and living is to proceed out of our own resources, asking God to add his blessing to our efforts. It's how we all tend to operate without even realizing it, even as born again believers. But it is backward. When you have a Lamborghini engine under the hood, it's odd to try to get your car going like Fred Flintstone, using the power of your own legs on

---

1   Edith Schaeffer, *The Tapestry: The Life and Times of Francis and Edith Schaeffer* (Waco, TX: Word, 1981), 356.

the ground. All the right doctrine, without fire and life, will only render us all the more open to judgment on the final day. Fire and life, energy and power, the very glimpse of heaven that we all long to be—this comes only to a life yielded wholeheartedly to the Spirit and his quiet, gracious, humble, risk-taking ways.

This final chapter reflects on the only way to make the previous eight chapters work in your life: keeping in step with the indwelling Spirit.

The Father ordains salvation, the Son accomplishes salvation, and the Spirit applies salvation. In other words, there is no Christian life without the Spirit. The Christian life is purely theoretical if there is no operation of the Spirit. Everything that we *experience* of God is the working of the Spirit. That is true at conversion, as the Spirit opens our eyes to our sin and Christ's saving offer. And it is true of our growth.

The main thing I want to say in this chapter is this: because of the Spirit, *you can grow*. You really can. Those feelings of futility, that sense of impossibility, the settled resignation that you have permanently plateaued—that is not of heaven but of hell. Satan loves your shrugged acquiescence to your sin. Jesus Christ's own heart for you is flourishing growth. He understands more deeply than you do the psychology of the heart fueling the sin you can't seem to leave behind once and for all. And he is well prepared and fully equipped to walk you out of that darkness. For he has given you the most precious gift of all: his own Holy Spirit. Everything said thus far in this book would remain purely abstract without the Spirit. It would all be fine theory, nothing more. The Spirit gives life, turning doctrine into power.

The Holy Spirit is how God gets inside you. If you are a Christian, you are now permanently indwelt by the Spirit, and if you are permanently indwelt by the Spirit, then you have been *supernaturalized*.

It's not just you anymore. You aren't alone. You have a companion living within you. He is there to stay, and he provides everything you need to grow in Christ.

If you choose to stay in your sins, you won't be able to stand before God one day and tell him he didn't provide you with the resources.

The New Age

In order to understand what the Holy Spirit does and how he empowers us to grow, we need first to understand where we are in human history.

When Jesus showed up, he said, "The time is fulfilled" (Mark 1:15). Paul said that "the end of the ages has come" (1 Cor. 10:11). Peter wrote that with the coming of Jesus we are "in the last times" (1 Pet. 1:20). John said, "It is the last hour" (1 John 2:18). Apparently the apostles all understood something momentous had happened on the scene of world history. What did they mean?

It's natural to think that all of human history is one fairly seamless storyline that will be brought to its decisive culmination one day when Jesus returns. But according to the Bible, the most decisive turning point in history has already happened. When Jesus came, and especially when he died and rose again, God was not simply providing salvation—he was also launching the new creation. The end of history, when Eden 2.0 would wash over this miserable world, was launched back into the middle of history. Does that sound like an overstatement? Think of it this way. What did the Old Testament anticipate taking place at the end of the world?

1. The ruinous fall into sin at Eden wrought by Adam would be undone.
2. God would make a new creation.

3. Sin and evil would be judged.

4. God would triumph once and for all over his enemies.

5. God's people would be vindicated.

6. The nations of the world would flock to Jerusalem.

7. Messiah would come.

8. The latter-day kingdom would be launched.

9. The dead would be raised.

When we get to the New Testament, we do not find the apostles joining in the Old Testament's anticipation of these final events—we find the apostles declaring that *every one of these hopes has been fulfilled.*

1. A second Adam has indeed triumphed in the same way that the first Adam fell—for example, both were tempted by Satan, one succumbing and the other not (Luke 3:38–4:13). And not only at the beginning of his ministry but throughout, Jesus has shown himself to be a successful Adam—Christ exorcised demons, for example, while Adam failed to drive Satan out of the garden.

2. God's new creation has indeed dawned (2 Cor. 5:17; Gal. 6:15).

3. Sin *was* once and for all judged in the crucifixion of Jesus. When Christ was crucified, he was experiencing the final end-time judgment, all funneled down onto a single man (Rom. 5:9; 1 Thess. 5:9).

4. As Jesus was crucified, God definitively triumphed over his enemies (Col. 2:13–15).

5. As the "justified," the people of God *have* been vindicated (Rom. 5:1). The declaration of "innocent" anticipated at the end of all things has been pronounced in the present based on a middle-of-history event.

6. The Gentiles are *now* flooding in as never before (Rom. 15:8–27).

7. Messiah *has* landed on the scene of human history (Rom. 1:3–4).

8. As Jesus himself said, the kingdom is here (Mark 1:15; cf. Acts 20:25; 28:31; Rom. 14:17). We are now *in* the last days (Heb. 1:2).

9. In Christ, the dead *have* been raised—not yet bodily, but spiritually, which is the hardest part. To be a Christian is to be one who has been "raised with Christ" (Eph. 2:6; Col. 3:1).

All this is glorious. But there's one more marker that the new age has dawned. Paired with the coming of the Messiah, it is the most significant one. *The Spirit would be poured out.* Geerhardus Vos demonstrated this in a seminal article called "The Eschatological Aspect of the Pauline Conception of the Spirit."[2] His point was that in Paul's theology, the descent of the Holy Spirit was *the* defining mark that the new age had been launched.

The Holy Spirit was active in Old Testament times, but selectively. The Spirit came upon Bezalel and Oholiab, for example, to equip them for the construction of the tabernacle in which God would dwell (Ex. 31:1–6). But in the New Testament, the Spirit comes upon all of God's people; they are *themselves* the tabernacle in which God dwells. The Spirit is a universal gift to all God's people. And the Spirit is the continuation, so to speak, of Jesus himself. Jesus spoke of his departure being necessary so that the Spirit could come (John 16:7; cf. 14:12–17). In the Spirit, we have something more wonderful than those who spoke and ate with Jesus himself. And this Spirit's arrival marks the dawning new creation.

---

2 Geerhardus Vos, "The Eschatological Aspect of the Pauline Conception of the Spirit," in *Redemptive History and Biblical Interpretation: The Shorter Writings of Geerhardus Vos*, ed. Richard B. Gaffin Jr. (Phillipsburg, NJ: Presbyterian and Reformed, 1980), 91–125.

The first thing to get straight, then, is that if you are a Christian, you have been plucked up out of the old age and placed into the new age. And the presence of the Spirit in your life is the proof. Sin and pain and futility continue in your life, because the presence of the new age did not eradicate the old age but overlaid it. This is why theologians speak of "the overlap of the ages." Rather than the old age stopping when the new age began, the new age began in the middle of the old age. When Jesus returns, then the old age will discontinue. But do not let the ongoing presence of the old age blind you to the wondrous inbreaking two thousand years ago of the new age.

You are an eschatological creature. To be sure, you won't be perfect in this life. We can't go thirty seconds freed of the mind's disease of Self informing what we think and desire. But there is no sin in your life more powerful than the Holy Spirit. There is nothing you can't beat. Your citizenship is now in heaven. You have an inner Friend who is prepared and equipped and ready now, right now, to walk you out of your darkest sin. Your spiritual ID card places your address, even now, in heaven.

Three Kinds of Men

One problem that may arise in your mind is that upright behavior actually seems quite doable without the Spirit. Are there not plenty of decent human beings who are not indwelt by the Spirit? Certainly. That is because all people are created in the image of God, and by God's universal common grace he restrains much evil that would otherwise be executed.

But still, you might wonder, do we really need the Spirit in order to live a moral life? The answer is that we do not need the Spirit to live a moral life, but we do need the Spirit to live a supernatural life. In other words, we don't need the Spirit to be different on the outside; we do need the Spirit to be different on the inside. Yet again: we don't need the Spirit to obey God; we do need the Spirit to *enjoy* obeying God. And that's the only kind of real obedience anyway, since enjoying God is itself one of God's commands (Deut. 28:47; Ps. 37:4; Phil. 4:4).

So we can stiff-arm God by breaking all the rules, or we can stiff-arm God by keeping all his rules but doing so begrudgingly.

C. S. Lewis brilliantly captures this in his little essay "Three Kinds of Men." He says that there are not two but three kinds of people in the world. The first consists of those who live purely for themselves, and all that they do serves their own selfish cares. The second kind are those who acknowledge that there is some code outside them that they should follow—whether conscience or the Ten Commandments or what their parents taught them or whatever. Lewis says that people of this second kind see this other moral claim on them but feel a tension between that external moral claim and their own natural desires. As a result they are constantly swiveling back and forth between pursuing their own desires and following this higher claim. Lewis insightfully relates this tension to that of paying a tax—people in this second category pay their taxes faithfully but hope that something will be left over for them to spend on themselves.

Some people throw out all rules (group 1). Others try to keep all the rules (group 2). Neither approach is New Testament Christianity. The third kind of person is operating on a different plane entirely. Lewis puts it like this:

> The third class is of those who can say like St Paul that for them "to live is Christ." These people have got rid of the tiresome business of adjusting the rival claims of Self and God by the simple expedient of rejecting the claims of Self altogether. The old egoistic will has

been turned round, reconditioned, and made into a new thing. The will of Christ no longer limits theirs; it is theirs. All their time, in belonging to Him, belongs also to them, for they are His.[3]

Lewis goes on to conclude that it is simplistic to view only two kinds of people, the disobedient and the obedient. For we can be "obedient" in the sense that we follow a certain code, yet in a taxpaying kind of way. The nuclear core of authentic Christianity is not simply doing what God says but enjoying God. "The price of Christ is something, in a way, much easier than moral effort—it is to want Him."[4]

The point of this book on growing in Christ is to help Christians leave behind the second kind of person Lewis describes here and to be melted, more and more deeply, into the third kind of person. And here's the point: we only get from person 2 to person 3 through the Holy Spirit. To grow as a disciple of Christ is not adding Christ *to* your life but collapsing into Christ *as* your life. He's not a new top priority, competing with the other claims of reputation, finances, and sexual gratification. He is asking you to embrace the freefall of total abandon to his purpose in your life. And that is why the Holy Spirit

---

3 C. S. Lewis, "Three Kinds of Men," in *Present Concerns* (London: Fount, 1986), 21. For similar articulations of what Lewis is after, though none quite as penetratingly clear as his, see Martin Luther, *Career of the Reformer III*, in *Luther's Works*, ed. Jaroslav Pelikan and Helmut T. Lehmann, 55 vols. (Philadelphia: Fortress, 1955–1986), 33:318; Luther, *The Christian in Society I*, in *Luther's Works*, 44:235–42 (cf. Luther, *Lectures on Galatians 1–4*, in *Luther's Works*, 26:125); Adolf Schlatter, *The Theology of the Apostles*, trans. Andreas J. Köstenberger (Grand Rapids, MI: Baker, 1997), 102; Geerhardus Vos, "Alleged Legalism in Paul," in Gaffin, *Redemptive History and Biblical Interpretation*, 390–92; F. B. Meyer, *The Directory of the Devout Life: Meditations on the Sermon on the Mount* (New York: Revell, 1904), 148–51; Herman Ridderbos, *Paul: An Outline of His Theology* (Grand Rapids, MI: Eerdmans, 1975), 137–40; Søren Kierkegaard, as quoted in Clare Carlisle, *Kierkegaard: A Guide for the Perplexed* (London: Continuum, 2007), 77–83; Martyn Lloyd-Jones, *Experiencing the New Birth: Studies in John 3* (Wheaton, IL: Crossway, 2015), 289.

4 Lewis, "Three Kinds of Men," 22.

dwells within you. He is the one who is empowering you to do what would be utterly impossible left to carnal resources—to step into the delicious, terrifying freedom of single-minded allegiance to Jesus.

It may feel impossible to you to do that. That's good. It *is* impossible. You'll never get there until you first try living for Christ out of your own strength and discover just how fearful and cautious and spiritually impotent you are on your own steam. It's then, as you give up on yourself and throw your hands up in the air, that your heart is most fertile for the supernaturalizing power of the Holy Spirit. For while the Spirit indwells every believer, we easily stifle his powerful work (Eph. 4:30).

Closed vents can't be cleaned, full cups can't be filled, and the Spirit does not enter where we are quietly operating out of self-dependence. But the distraught, the empty, the pleading, the self-despairing, those tired of paying the tax of obedience to God and trying to live on what's left over—theirs are hearts irresistible to the humble Holy Spirit.

Redirecting Our Gaze

How, though? How does the Holy Spirit actually propel inner change in Christians?

The main answer the New Testament gives us is: the Spirit changes us by making Christ wonderful to us. The third person of the Trinity does his work by spotlighting the second person of the Trinity.

Some quarters of the church focus on the Holy Spirit. Rightly sensing the neglect of the Spirit in some wings of the church, they make the Spirit the dominating center point. "It is the Spirit who gives life" (John 6:63), we are told. "To set the mind on the Spirit is life and peace" (Rom. 8:6).

Other quarters of the church emphasize Christ—"Him we pro-claim" (Col. 1:28), we are reminded. "We preach Christ" (1 Cor. 1:23).

But true apostolic Christianity understands that to diminish either the second or the third person of the Trinity is necessarily to diminish the other. For the Spirit himself fixes our gaze on Christ. The two work in tandem. The Spirit and Christ rise or diminish together. Let me show you this briefly in three passages of Scripture.

First, throughout John 14–16, Jesus comforts the disciples by teaching them that it is good for them that he will go away, so that the Spirit can come. And how does Jesus describe the work of the Spirit? The Spirit "will bear witness about" Jesus (15:26). The Spirit "will glorify" Jesus (16:13–14). The third person puts the second person in the foreground. The Spirit's animating impulse is not a raw, faceless power in the life of the Christian. The Spirit ignites our contemplation of Jesus Christ. The subjective work of the Spirit works in tandem with the objective work of Christ.

Second, remember 1 Corinthians 2:12, which I mentioned in pass-ing in chapter 4: "We have received not the spirit of the world, but the Spirit who is from God, that we might understand the things freely given us by God." We receive the Spirit, this text says, *in order that* we might grasp what we have freely received—the phrase "freely given" is one Greek word, formed out of the verb form (*charizomai*) of the noun for "grace" (*charis*). The Spirit opens our eyes to see what we have been "graced" with. And in keeping with the strongly Christocentric context of 1 Corinthians 2, both before and after verse 12, the Spirit opens our eyes to see what we have been graced with in Christ.

Third, and explicitly picking up the "seeing" metaphor I've been using in this chapter, remember what Paul says in 2 Corinthians 3:18, where he speaks of "beholding the glory of the Lord" ("Lord" being

Jesus in this context). Paul's point is that this very beholding of Jesus fundamentally transforms believers. But notice what Paul then says: all this "comes from the Lord who is the Spirit" (not a conflation of Christ and the Spirit but simply a most intimate association [cf. Rom. 8:9–11]). In brief: the Spirit effectually causes us to behold Christ in such a way that transforms us.

My burden in raising these three texts is to prevent you from trying to walk in the power of the Holy Spirit as some exercise separate from everything else I have been saying about focusing on Jesus Christ. Chapter 9 of this book is not shooting off in a new direction. The Holy Spirit clinches everything said in the first eight chapters. Be so radically Spirit-led that you are therefore radically Christ-centered. Christ and Spirit, the incarnate Son and the indwelling Spirit—this is your double gift.

Don't focus too much on the Spirit himself—focus on Christ, asking the Spirit to make Christ beautiful. The Spirit is the effectual cause of your growth, but Christ is the object to contemplate in your growth. A man doesn't focus on his brain when he looks at his wife and ponders how beautiful she is. He focuses on her and enjoys her. His brain is what effectually causes that enjoyment. But what would he say to someone who said he's been neglecting his brain by being so wife-centered? He'd say, *If it weren't for my brain, I would not be able to enjoy my wife at all. Praise God for a brain. But I don't look* at *my brain; I look* with *my brain.*

A Foretaste of Heaven

Keep in step with the person of the Holy Spirit. Ask the Father to fill you with the Spirit. Look to Christ, in the power of the Spirit. Open yourself up to the Spirit. Consecrate yourself to the beautiful Spirit's ways in your life. Recognize and believe way down deep in your heart that without the empowering Spirit all your ministry and efforts and evangelizing and attempts to kill sin will be in vain.

As you do so, you will be a little walking portrait of heaven itself to everyone around you. With lots of foibles and mistakes, for sure. And many lapses back into walking in the flesh—like Lewis's second kind of man. But here and there, at first for short bursts but gradually for longer stretches of your day, you will be learning to operate out of God's own divine resources. You will be leaving in your wake the irresistible flavor of heaven. For you will be giving people a taste of Jesus himself, the Lord whose Spirit has taken up residence within you.

Conclusion: What Now?

THE FINAL CONCLUSION, the deepest secret, to growing in Christ is this: look to him. Set your gaze upon him. Abide in him, hour by hour. Draw strength from his love. He is a person, not a concept. Become personally acquainted with him, ever more deeply as the years roll by. As the Scottish pastor Andrew Bonar said in an 1875 letter at age sixty-five: "Christ grows more precious every day. O to know His heart of love."[1]

It may seem, at this point in the book, that its nine chapters have given you a list of nine strategies to implement or nine different techniques to bear in mind. That's not at all what I want ringing in your heart as you close this short book. I do not have nine things to say. I have one thing to say. Look to Christ. You will grow in Christ as you direct your gaze to Christ. If you take your eyes off of Jesus Christ and direct your gaze to your own growth, you will prevent the very growth you desire.

On September 10, 1760, John Newton wrote to a "Miss Med-hurst," who was one of a group of women Newton had visited in

---

1   In Marjory Bonar, ed., *Reminiscences of Andrew A. Bonar* (London: Hodder and Stoughton, 1897), 224.

Yorkshire to offer spiritual counsel. Responding to her and her friends' request for help in going deeper with the Lord, he said:

> The best advice I can send, or the best wish I can form for you, is that you may have an abiding and experimental sense of those words of the apostle which are just now upon my mind—"*Looking unto Jesus*." The duty, the privilege, the safety, the unspeakable happiness, of a believer, are all comprised in that one sentence. . . . Looking unto Jesus is the object that melts the soul into love and gratitude.[2]

My goal in this book has simply been to coach you into that single, simple, all-determining impulse of the heart: looking to Jesus. If you look to him, everything else is footnotes. All else will fall into place. If you do not look to Jesus, no amount of techniques or strategies will finally help you; all will be for nothing. Peel back every layer of distraction and look to Christ. Simplify your heart and all its cares. Look to Christ and his overflowing heart.

The nine chapters of this book are not sequential steps in growing; they are different facets of the one diamond of growth. In order to grow, we need to see who the real Jesus is (chap. 1), collapsing into his arms and continuing to do so all our lives long (chap. 2) as those united to him (chap. 3), drinking down his undeserved love (chap. 4) and full legal exoneration on the basis of his own finished work (chap. 5), being therefore freed up to walk in the light (chap. 6) and receive the anguish of this life as the gentle hand of God to help us rather than to punish us (chap. 7), seeing the love of Christ by inhaling the Bible and returning our love to him in exhaled prayer

2 *Letters of John Newton* (Edinburgh: Banner of Truth, 2007), 47–48.

(chap. 8), and actually experiencing the love of heaven through the indwelling Spirit (chap. 9). This is a book with one point: Be astonished at the gracious heart of Jesus Christ, proven in his atoning work in the past and his endless intercession in the present. Receive his unutterable love for sinners and sufferers. Stop resisting. Let him draw near to you. Gaze upon him.

As you do so, transformation will come in the back door. If you try to change simply for change's sake, you can only change your behavior. You can't change your heart. But mere behavioral change isn't change at all. Peel your eyes away from yourself—even your change or lack thereof—and ponder Christ. Commune with him. Open the vent of your heart. Receive his love and counsel from Scripture. See him in the preached word and sacrament at your local church. Look at him. Stare.

This single focus is why I have not sought to be exhaustive in this short book. I have said virtually nothing about some important facets of our spiritual growth—the Sabbath, for example, or small groups, or fasting, or the local church, or several other important elements of healthy Christian discipleship. Instead, I have asked the question: what must happen in the individual human heart, most fundamentally, most deeply, for a man or woman to get traction and grow? And the message of this book is that *the* way we grow is receiving the heartful love of Jesus. The gospel of grace not only gets us in but moves us along. Other books will be needed to supplement this one. But they are downstream of this one. Without the conviction of this book in place, none of the others will avail.

So let your union and communion with Jesus Christ, the friend of sinners, take you deeper, ever deeper, into the wonders of the gospel. And watch your heart, and therefore your whole life, blossom.

Learn much of the Lord Jesus. For every look at yourself, take ten looks at Christ. He is altogether lovely. Such infinite majesty, and yet such meekness and grace, and all for sinners, even the chief! Live much in the smiles of God. Bask in his beams. Feel his all-seeing eye settled on you in love, and repose in his almighty arms. . . . Let your soul be filled with a heart-ravishing sense of the sweetness and excellency of Christ and all that is in Him. Let the Holy Spirit fill every chamber of your heart; and so there will be no room for folly, or the world, or Satan, or the flesh.[3]

3 Robert Murray McCheyne, in an 1840 letter, in Andrew A. Bonar, *Memoirs and Remains of the Rev. Robert Murray McCheyne* (Edinburgh: Oliphant, Anderson, and Ferrier, 1892), 293.

Acknowledgments

THANK YOU, MIKE REEVES, for inviting me to contribute this book to the Union series. This partnership, and the friendship it reflects, is precious to me.

Thank you, Davy Chu, Drew Hunter, and Wade Urig, brother pastors whom I revere, for reading and improving the manuscript. I love you.

Thank you, dearest Stacey, for insisting that I keep writing and for encouraging me all along the way. I adore you.

Thank you, Crossway, for your care of this project from start to finish.

Thank you, Thom Notaro, for your wonderful partnership in this project as its editor.

I dedicate this book to my seminary professors. When I landed on the campus of Covenant Theological Seminary in St. Louis in August 2002, I could hardly believe what I was seeing: men of God whose erudition and learning and commitment to the doctrines of grace *took them down deeper into humility and love*. I could have learned Greek anywhere; I could only learn interpersonal beauty fueled by Reformed theology at Covenant, under the faculty who were there at that time. They gave me a theological foundation for understanding how I grow as a Christian. But then, more wondrously, they gave me living pictures of what such growth blossoms into. In this Mordor of a world, I found myself in the Shire. What a mercy for God to send me there. I needed it. I still do. Thank you, dear fathers and brothers.

General Index

abiding in Christ, 171
acquittal, 85–110
Adam, Thomas, 92
adoption, 91
  as familial metaphor, 63
Aesop's Fables approach (Bible reading), 150
affections, 77
affliction, 133. *See also* pain
alien righteousness, 86
aloneness, 118
appearance of godliness, 90, 115, 118
Augustine, 17, 41

Bavinck, Herman, 17, 93
behavior, 17
behavior modification, 18
Belgic Confession, 93–94
Berkouwer, G. C., 93
Bible
  corrects us, 145–46
  divine authorship of, 147
  as good news, 148–51
  Jesus walks across its pages, 78
  original languages of, 147–48
  oxygenates us, 146, 156
  preciousness of, 144

Bible reading
  as daily ritual, 151–52
  as inhaling, 143–52, 156
  wrong ways to read, 149–50
bodily resurrection, 127
body of Christ, 112
Bonar, Andrew, 171
Bonhoeffer, Dietrich, 114–15
breathing, 27, 143–57
Bridges, Jerry, 53n2
Bunyan, John, 17, 73
Burroughs, Jeremiah, 51–52

Calvin, John, 17
  on the Psalms, 155–56
  on union with Christ, 62
Campbell, Constantine R., 57n6
Camp Ridgecrest (North Carolina), 120–21
Canons of Dort, 94
Chalmers, Thomas, 93
Christian life
  as avoiding pain, 125
  as curved down to death and up to resurrection life, 44
  defined by love of God, 83
  gospel as sustaining reality, 98–99
  and Holy Spirit, 160

Scripture Index

Union

We fuel reformation in churches and lives.

Union Publishing invests in the next generation of leaders with theology that gives them a taste for a deeper knowledge of God. From books to our free online content, we are committed to producing excellent resources that will refresh, transform, and grow believers and their churches.

We want people everywhere to know, love, and enjoy God, glorifying him in everything they do. For this reason, we've collected hundreds of free articles, podcasts, book chapters, and video content for our free online collection. We also produce a fresh stream of written, audio, and video resources to help you to be more fully alive in the truth, goodness, and beauty of Jesus.

If you are hungry for reformational resources that will help you delight in God and grow in Christ, we'd love for you to visit us at unionpublishing.org.

unionpublishing.org

Union Series

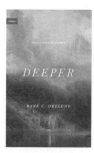

FULL EDITION
Rejoice and Tremble

CONCISE EDITION
What Does It Mean to Fear the Lord?

FULL EDITION
Deeper

CONCISE EDITION
How Does God Change Us?

The Union series invites readers to experience deeper enjoyment of God through four interconnected values: delighting in God, growing in Christ, serving the church, and blessing the world.

For more information, visit **crossway.org**.